SO YOU WANT TO BE A
PRINCIPAL

Musings of a Public and
International School Administrator

W. FRED BOWEN

Copyright © 2022 W. Fred Bowen.

All rights reserved. No part of this book may be reproduced, stored, or transmitted by any means—whether auditory, graphic, mechanical, or electronic—without written permission of both publisher and author, except in the case of brief excerpts used in critical articles and reviews. Unauthorized reproduction of any part of this work is illegal and is punishable by law.

ISBN: 979-8-88640-100-4 (sc)
ISBN: 979-8-88640-101-1 (hc)
ISBN: 979-8-88640-102-8 (e)

Because of the dynamic nature of the Internet, any web addresses or links contained in this book may have changed since publication and may no longer be valid. The views expressed in this work are solely those of the author and do not necessarily reflect the views of the publisher, and the publisher hereby disclaims any responsibility for them.

One Galleria Blvd., Suite 1900, Metairie, LA 70001
1-888-421-2397

This book is dedicated to my wife, Tanya, who stands by me through the good and bad times and who, as well as anyone, understands the role of the principal.

CONTENTS

Acknowledgements vii
Foreword ix
Preface xi

PART 1

Chapter 1 Death 3
   My First Dance 3
   Graduating Class 6
   Bicycle 8
   Stabbing 10
   Suicide 11
   Accidental 14
   Automobile Accident 16
   Nigerian Public Execution 17
   Russian Deaths 19
   Natural Death in Saudi Arabia 21

Chapter 2 Assault 23
   Knife Incident 23
   Love and Hate 25
   Hit the Principal 27
   Teacher Hits Student 28
   Teacher Grabs Student 29
   Parent Slaps Teacher 30
   Parent Threatens Teacher 31

  Hockey Player Threatens Student Body.................................32
  Big Boy Assaults Little Boy..34
  Weapons at Dance..35

Chapter 3 Humor.. 37
  Shop Teacher Prank 37
  Fire Extinguisher Safety 38
  Loss of Virginity..39
  Teacher Masturbation 41

Chapter 4 Illegal.. 44
  Crime in School 44
  K-9 Policemen 46
  Six Burglars..47
  Safe Safe? 49
  Blue Dye 50
  Teachers Steal Too...51

Chapter 5 Drugs..53
  Desks 53
  Parking Lot Busts 54
  Hash Knives...54

Chapter 6 Alcohol.. 56
  Martini Lunch 56
  Drunk at the Dance 57

Chapter 7 Awkward and Difficult... 59
  Vandalism 59
  Neighborhood Cleanup..61
  Christmas Concert Meltdown 63
  Nervous Breakdown 65
  Inappropriate Relationship 66
  Leadership..69

PART 2

Chapter 8   International Education – Nigeria 75
   Nigerian Administrative Experience 75
   Airport Bribery 76
   Living in Nigeria 78
   The University of Jos 78
   Popcorn Snacks 80
   Western Shopping 81
   Teaching at University 82
   More Bribery 83

Chapter 9   International Education – Russia 88
   Administration in Moscow 88
   Replacing a Disgruntled Principal 89
   School Security in Moscow 90
   Security Stress 91
   Expatriate Parents 92
   Family Issues 93
   My Son, the Fighter 94
   Diverse Culture Issues 95
   My Daughter Meets the Queen 96

Chapter 10 International Education – Saudi Arabia 99
   Administration in Saudi Arabia 99
   Shipment and Saudi Bureaucracy 100
   Political Contacts 103
   Religious Police 105
   Burglary 106
   Wall Extension 109
   Public Meeting Embarrassment 110
   Hand-Holding Onstage 113
   Christmas Concert—An International Incident 115

United Nations Transgression 116
Church Steeples are a No-No 117
Crown Prince Visit 118
High School Start-up 120

Chapter 11 District Office Administration 121
Assistant Superintendent Human Resources...........................121
Alcohol and Caning 122
Cultural and Racial Bias...125
Demonstration Against the West...126
Security in the Kingdom 128
Attack at School 130
Attack at the Petroleum Center 135
Attack at Housing Compound 138
School Closures 143
Government Interference...145
Supervision and Evaluation 148

Chapter 12 The End of a Career 151
Culminating Events 151
Some Final Thoughts 163

ACKNOWLEDGEMENTS

The incidents cited in this book are true. I have changed the names of most persons involved and many of the site descriptions are purposefully vague. Nevertheless, all of the events were witnessed by me at first hand—most while I was engaged as a school principal or superintendent, and some that occurred while I was teaching in the schools. In each instance, the skills and techniques necessary to deal with the situations had never been explained, taught nor even mentioned by superiors—the situations necessitated true on-the-job training. The impact on the administrators mentioned was significant personal and professional stress; sometimes mistakes were made and people suffered, but powerful lessons were learned.

I would like to acknowledge the thousands of students and teachers with whom I have worked over the course of my twenty-eight years as a school administrator. It is my association with them that has motivated me to record the events of this book. I also wish to thank my family who, while living through many of the experiences cited here, also had to live with me when I came home.

FOREWORD

My years as a school principal were perhaps the most challenging, difficult and, yet, rewarding periods of my professional life. I was fortunate as an administrator to work at all levels of education, from pre-school through twelfth grade and even into adult education and university. During these often tense and difficult times, I would occasionally question my own motivation for remaining in school administration—but then, the intrinsic rewards of working with young people would usher me back to reality and the joys of being an educator and administrator.

In *So You Want To Be a Principal*, I try to accurately recite the events as they took place and to explain their impact on me, the teachers with whom I worked and the students. After the passage of many years, it is easy to glorify or embellish situational events, but I have seriously tried to report details as they happened and, where appropriate, describe the impact on me and others.

As you read the incidents, you will note that they are not necessarily in chronological order, but in fact are described under the chapter headings in which they most appropriately fit. However the first occurred when I was a spanking new teacher in 1966 and the final took place during my final year working as an educational administrator--2006. It may be possible to notice trends in behavior and the evolution of my educational thought processes during the reading. The incidents described encompass more than forty years of work in schools—surely sufficient time for professional philosophies and personal biases to develop.

This book has two distinct parts; the first recounts predominantly the situations I experienced in public schools in the United States and Canada. The second describes the issues and circumstances surrounding my career as an educational administrator in international schools in foreign countries.

Finally, it is my hope that you will find entertainment, motivation and empathy in the stories I have to tell; those of you who aspire to become a principal—maybe this will give you some second thoughts—or maybe it will inspire you to rise to the administrative challenge that is so much needed in schools of today.

PREFACE

The evolution of formal education has been a gradual process during the past century. One need only consider the similarities between my generation's classroom experiences and those of my parents. My father often described the rigor and pedantic nature of his learning, but described at the same time typical classrooms, replete with rows of desks, black-boarded wall, teachers' desks in the front of classrooms and a wall of windows. Teacher lectures, class work, oral presentations, exams, homework and textbooks seem to have been present in much the same form as well. It is only with the advent of technology—calculators, audio-visual presentations, computers—that major differences have become significantly evident. The basic formula for learning: teacher lecture, textbook confirmation, student practice and the testing of accumulated knowledge continues to permeate our school classrooms and the overall learning process.

The role of teacher has therefore also been a slowly evolving process. As evidenced by the nature of teacher preparation and certification courses presented in universities and teacher colleges of yore, together with certification requirements of the present, teachers with similar characteristics and skills have continued to be produced.

What about the administrators? Has this snail-like evolution had little impact on the role of school administrators as well? The obvious role of the school-based administrator has evolved too. Someone must prepare school budgets, create teaching schedules, work out classroom schedules (i.e. gymnasiums, art rooms, science labs, libraries, music rooms, etc.), correlate school bus operations, control extra-curricular activities including sports, fine arts performances and displays, graduation ceremonies and community involvement projects. Oh, and of course, provide for overall school discipline, including policies and final judgments/punishments, supervision of instruction in all classrooms and disciplines and provide evaluation of teacher and staff performance. And one must not forget the initiation and on-going administration of curriculum projects including development, implementation and evaluation—which may or may not affect the actual learning of students. Overseeing the continuing professional development of teachers, the effective communication between home and school, the inception and administration of parent-teacher groups, and negotiations with professional teacher organizations must be the responsibility of the administrator as well. And, overall maintenance of the physical plants, including classrooms, hallways, wash rooms, gymnasiums, offices, cafeterias, work rooms, libraries, auditoriums, shops, not to mention the external areas—landscaping athletic field, playgrounds, parking lots and out-buildings. And who ensures that the bills are paid, the payrolls are met, persons are hired and fired, that expenses don't exceed budgets and expense correlates with quality education? The administrators, of course.

It seems highly unlikely that this wide-ranging conglomeration of responsibilities was originally recognized and assigned to school administration. However, then like now, someone had to do it. The role of the school administrator has continued to expand and increase ever since.

"No problem!" one might say. Universities will prepare potential school vice-principals, principals, superintendents, as well as curriculum coordinators, directors and department heads for these roles--NOT! Sadly, and in some cases tragically, university courses cannot prepare the prospective administration in all these areas. Believe it or not, most effective administrator training is on-the-job training. School administrators learn as they go. Most have studied such things as budgeting and budget control, learning and leadership styles—even time tabling, but it is painfully obvious that the effective administrator must move well beyond these to bring excellence into the performance of his/her role.

The administrative role in schools of today is a blended role (some would say confused) between corporate leader and humanitarian miracle worker—between firm disciplinarian and sensitive "friend"/counselor—between arbiter and "deal maker"—between supervisor and co-worker. Should the administrator be deficient in any of these areas, his/her role and ability to fulfill these obligations and responsibilities will be misconstrued and misunderstood by most outside observers.

So, in summary, where does one learn to understand and effectively carry out these roles—on the job! The administrator must bring strong professional and personal characteristics to the role, or he/she will be destined to fail.

As a functioning school administrator, although I had completed the requisite university requirements to be certified as a teacher, I had never been near a course in educational administration. Moving up the ladder of responsibility in schools in the 1960's, 70's, 80's and even the 90's was usually the result of strong capabilities as a teacher in the classroom combined with an expressed wish to become an administrator. There were no required classes—no specific preparation for the position—just the personal characteristics of an effective teacher and the desire to become an administrator.

Obviously today, many jurisdictions require all prospective school administrators to prepare themselves in "school administration" classes. Once they have the administration certification completed, they are prepared—at least in the pedantic, bureaucratic sense to become a school leader.

In this book, I relate for you many of the genuine experiences I had over the years which made me into the administrator I became. In most cases, the learning which I amassed through the on-the-job real training was what propelled me to the levels of administrative professionalism I obtained. As I look back and consider the outcomes and results of my activities over the years, I wonder about the affect on the thousands of students and hundreds of teachers with whom I worked. Could I have been better trained—undoubtedly. Could the stresses of administration been less with better preparation—without question.

This leads me to the overall thesis of this book…do you really wish to become a school administrator?

PART 1

DEATH

My First Dance

In 1967, I began my career in education as a high school teacher. My first teaching position was at a well-known high school in Hawaii. It was a large school, with several buildings on a large campus. I was excited just to be working with students, and the opportunity to work in the island paradise was "a dream come true." Unfortunately, during this particular time, the use and abuse of drugs was becoming prevalent in schools in the United States.

I volunteered to return to the campus on a Friday evening in October of that year to supervise the first student dance of the year. I had only attended school dances prior to that time as a student, and was therefore unsure of what to expect. The dance was held in a large cafeteria building, chairs and tables moved to the sides of the room. I of course arrived early and was at the door as the students began to enter the building. They were excited and loud, looking forward to the first dance of the year and the opportunity to meet their friends and renew old acquaintances. The weather dictated the dress in Hawaii, and the students were dressed mostly in shorts and t-shirts. The girls were naturally better dressed, in their 'special' outfits, than the boys. It was obvious that the dance was going to be well attended as students streamed into the building in a seeming unending rush. The music was provided by a local 'DJ' service and included all of the popular music of the day. Immediately, the dance floor filled with jumping and gyrating bodies. The students surely knew how to dance. Within minutes, the heat and humidity of the evening became noticeable and somewhat oppressing. That didn't seem to bother the dancers, however, and very soon their brows, backs, necks and clothing were covered in sweat. No matter, they were having a super time and the dance was going well.

As a new teacher, I was unsure what my duties consisted of, and so I began to move about the dance floor and observe the students to see what I could see. Perhaps I would see something to supervise. Other teachers and the school vice principal were also supervising, and they seemed to be doing the same as I.

Within the first hour of the dance, I began to notice individual students and one particularly tall, attractive and energetic girl caught my eye. She had not paused from the moment she arrived and was dancing and jumping and moving with high energy. It didn't seem to me that she had a date, and often, perhaps not even a dance partner, but she danced without pause. I noticed her because of the unusually high energy she possessed. I began to notice that every few minutes, she would rush off of the dance floor and, with other girls, would go into the girls' restroom. Because the visits seemed so frequent, I assumed she was trying to minimize the amount of sweat pouring down her face and body—it made sense to me.

After each of about four or five visits to the restroom, she reappeared on the dance floor and went wildly crazy. I was observing her return to the dance floor, when, without warning, she collapsed to floor. I immediately moved in her direction as the floor was crowded with bodies and I was afraid she might be hurt. I immediately began to yell at students to move away from her, expecting that she would recover and stand up. The vice-principal too had seen her fall and approached her from the other side. She looked as if she had fainted and he knelt down to assist her. It was at that moment, that he and I both saw blood. A lot of blood. She was bleeding from her nose, mouth and ears! I immediately enlisted the aid of several students who were near, and had them help me to form a circle around her and the vice principal. The amount of blood was frightening. The vice-principal by this time had her head in his lap—he was seated on the floor—and blood was beginning to pool around them. By now, the girl had been on the floor three or four minutes and it appeared that she was not going to regain consciousness. Another teacher rushed to the telephone and called an ambulance.

The rest of the time until the girl had been taken away in the ambulance was a blur. Students were crying, teachers were shouting and the scene was bedlam. We began to move the students out of the building and away from the disturbing scene on the floor. When it was over—the rest of the dance evening was cancelled--and the students had gone home, we learned what had happened. The dancing girl and her friends were going into the restroom to "get high". They had secreted a spray can of a furniture polish with them into the restroom. There, they sprayed the contents onto paper towels, sniffed the fumes and headed back out to the dance floor.

The information that came back to the school days later indicated that the blood vessels in the girl's lungs had ruptured, causing her to bleed to death.

Such was the occasion of my first dance supervision—a harbinger perhaps for many other difficult experiences to come during the next forty years. Experiencing this tragic event obviously had a deep impact on me and my future years as an administrator. Observing the joys of being young and yet realizing that there has to be a balance between experiencing joy and behaving with common sense and decorum became significant principles for me. It was never far from my mind that inappropriate behaviors could easily lead to tragedy. Perhaps this realization made me less willing to "look the other way" when student behavior was questionable during the many student activities I observed, supervised and participated in the years to come.

Graduating Class

It seems like only yesterday when I was a relatively new teacher teaching high school in a small town in Alberta, Canada. I had completed my studies at university and gained a Master of Arts Degree, and had, out of financial necessity taken a teaching job in this small, but exciting community. The high school was called a composite high school, because, in addition to offering a normal, academic diploma, it also offered a wide-range of vocational programs leading to employment after high school. Further, the high school served the needs of students who lived on farms in the surrounding countryside, who, although they had elementary schools in their immediate community, had to travel to the 'larger' center to attend high school. These circumstances led to an exciting and lively student body of more than five hundred students, energized by their associations and relationships, and characterized by their participation in inter-school athletics which had been impossible in the smaller centers.

It was during my third year teaching in this school that a severely tragic event took place. The graduating class of 1973 was anxiously awaiting graduation at the end of May. As is so often the case in rural schools, the Grade 12 Graduation Committee was composed of students who lived in a variety of locations, many of them on farms located in the area. Another characteristic of this particular graduating committee was that it was predominantly female—no editorializing here. At any rate, in the second week of May, this committee was holding a regularly scheduled meeting at the home of one of its members. She happened to live on a farm which was some distance from the school, but had volunteered her home as the venue for this meeting. Transportation could have been a concern, but in those days it was normal for many of our students to have driving privileges because of rural living requirements. One of the girls volunteered her boyfriend to drive herself and four other girls to the meeting. They met after school and, packing five girls plus the driver into the car, headed out of town.

It so happened in those days that rural Alberta was served by a minimal rail service; that is, a one car train, often referred to locally as a "bumble car", complete with its own locomotion, traveled from the larger cities such as Calgary and Edmonton to the rural areas. These "bumble cars" traveled at relatively high speeds on the rails, and most, but not all, railroad crossings were controlled. The uncontrolled crossings were those where the train lines crossed small gravel roads between communities. Obviously, rural people had become used to these trains traveling through the countryside; this is good and bad. Most people understood the potential dangers associated with the trains, and therefore respected their passage through the country. Sometimes, accidents would happen for this very reason, as farmers working in tractors with enclosed cabs, would occasionally forget about the trains, and not hearing the rumble of the wheels, would inadvertently pull across the tracks at just the wrong time.

This early evening, the students in the car were presumably not concerned or thinking about "bumble cars" and uncontrolled crossings. In fact, after the accident, all indications are that the driver of the vehicle either attempted to beat the train to the crossing as evidenced by the high rate of speed at which the car was traveling, or he was unaware of the approaching disaster. At any rate, there was a collision at the crossing and all five of the high school students and the driver were killed instantly. Such a tragic accident in a high school graduating class of approximately one hundred students is not an experience easily forgotten.

There were six separate funerals the next week and the graduating ceremonies at the end of the month were tragically impacted by the memory of the loss of classmates and friends.

Tragedy is never far away when dealing with large numbers of young persons. As a school administrator, one should be prepared to deal with such devastating events and have plans and procedure in place. The psychological and emotional well-being of students and faculty cannot be under-valued.

Bicycle

While teaching in rural Alberta, Canada, during my early years of teaching, I got to know a young neighbor, who I will call Bill. I was teaching high school at the time, and Bill was probably still in elementary school. He and his brother and parents became good neighborhood friends and we spoke often. Imagine my surprise, when, several years later, as an administrator in a high school in a larger city, I was greeted by Bill. He informed me that his family too had moved to the city and that he would be attending the school where I worked.

Bill was not a super student—in fact, just the opposite. He rarely worked hard and consequently found a lot of ways to get into trouble. I eventually assigned him as an advisee in my advisor group, in order to keep closer track of him and as a favor to his parents. He was a drummer and excelled in music classes at the school. He played in a rock and roll band and this encouraged him to remain in school and, all signs indicated, he would eventually graduate from high school.

In his Grade 12 year, Bill was still in school and still very active in music classes. He had had some trouble with the police and school administration, but was a super boy—very likeable and personable. One evening, he was returning home fairly late on his bicycle; I don't know where he had been. As fate would have it, a young woman who had been out drinking was also returning home that night. She was drunk, but was behind the wheel and driving with undue care. Somehow, she ran into Bill and his bicycle, and although the collision didn't kill him outright, after she had dragged him a significant distance, and then left him bleeding beside the street, Bill bled to death. The young woman drove to her home, which was not far away, parked her damaged car in her garage, and went to bed. She did not stop to try and help Bill nor did she call an ambulance or report the accident. When Bill was found later that night, he was dead.

It took several days and an extensive police investigation for the police to finally discover that it was this particular young woman who had run Bill down. Of course, there was a court case, and she was found guilty of manslaughter, due mainly to the condition of her car which was damaged in such a way as to prove it was the instrument of death.

Bill's funeral was a very sad affair, held in the church just down the street from the high school. Bill's band played the music and Bill's music teacher gave the eulogy. The school faculty, administration and student body mourned his passing for a considerable period of time. All students, including those whose lives are difficult and who do not endear themselves to the teachers and administrators in school, are vulnerable. Tragedy is no respecter of persons and all students should receive equal levels of respect and consideration—no one can predict who will suffer in life.

Stabbing

Our high school was located in a part of the city where the housing subdivisions were fairly new. The city planners had, in addition to planning school locations in the community, also laid out parks and green strips that would make living in these subdivisions more pleasant and attractive. The high school practice fields were large and conducive to attracting onlookers for athletic events and practices.

One afternoon, a substantial group of young persons had gathered near the practice fields to 'hang out' after school. A young male student, part of the larger group, stayed after school on that afternoon to be a part of the crowd. Sometime later, he had a verbal altercation with another boy, as high school boys often do, and decided it was better to head for home than to have a fight. He took off, walking across the practice field and then continuing down one of the park-like green strips, heading in the direction of his home.

Unaware that he was being followed, he was within a short distance of his home, when he was confronted by the boy with whom he had had the earlier confrontation. The boy, together with some of his friends, had decided that a fight was the only way to settle the disagreement. The boys formed a circle, as they do, and then pushed the two antagonists together to settle their disagreement with fisticuffs. After a lot of yelling and pushing, the boys exchanged blows. The aggressor, getting the worst of the fight, reached into his pocket and pulled out a knife. Now, it wasn't a big knife—in fact the knife blade was perhaps no more than an inch in length—about the length of a little finger. According to the boy later, he pulled the knife to "scare" the other boy. At any rate, he jabbed at him a couple of times, and then, was amazed to see the boy fall to the ground. The boy appeared to be in some pain, but there was no physical damage to be seen.

Some of the onlookers became frightened and took off running. Fortunately, a woman who had observed the fracas from her kitchen window had already called the police, who arrived shortly thereafter. They approached the boy on the ground and discovered he was in severe distress. An ambulance was called and the boy was rushed to the hospital. There it was discovered that the short blade of the knife had, when jabbed in the boy's direction, penetrated the chest just above the heart. The small blade had conveniently slipped between the ribs and nicked the top of the heart and the arteries connected there. The boy bled to death internally.

Weapons, no matter how insignificant, have no place in schools. Young persons, products of a modern society which has often blurred the consequences of violence through movies, video games, sports, wars, etc., need to be educated regarding possible consequences of violent action. Administrators cannot ignore the need for schools to pick up the responsibility for teaching our youth the potential horrors of unthinking violence.

Suicide

As a relatively new principal of a junior high school, I had several experiences that were poignant learning experiences for me. One of the more difficult episodes began when I took a particularly disruptive and, yet, bright student into my group of students with whom I worked and counseled personally. This young lad, probably 13 years of age, first came to my attention in a German class that I taught. (As a principal, teaching was not a part of my district assignment, but it was the one opportunity each day that allowed me some respite from the stresses of administration—and I loved it.) The boy was a failure in many ways; he was different in personality and in behavior from his peers. The other students did not understand him and frequently did not accept him as one of them. He was small in stature and physically defensive in most student confrontations—whether in the classroom or on the school grounds. However, he was an excellent German student. It was not long before his efforts in German language acquisition made him stand out in the class—a situation which he did not particularly like. Nevertheless, inasmuch as he was continually being sent to the office because of misbehaviors in other classes and other situational circumstances during the normal school day, I began to spend considerable time with him.

Our principal/student relationship developed into a mutually comfortable circumstance for both of us. He began to confide in me and was, at least on occasion, willing to discuss the difficulties of his young life with me. We spent, over the course of the school year, many hours together, working to make school life tolerable for him. He told me about his occasional living on the street—breaking into an abandoned commercial building in the middle of the city where he, together with many other young people, would eat and sleep and do drugs. He had a home, but was not particularly happy there, and frequently did not go home. His parent had given up on control in his young life years earlier and accepted him when he was around and didn't ask too many questions when he was not. Life was not easy. Our conversations at school seemed to bring him some satisfaction and his recognition that he was good at something, in this case learning the German language, gave him some self-respect and confidence.

During one particularly interesting meeting, he told me about his involvement, albeit somewhat superficial as he put it, with a coven of witches. Witchcraft in those years in the mid-seventies seemed to have a significant attraction for many young people. He claimed to have been invited on several occasions to participate with other young people in rites and rituals that represented witchcraft. Near the end of that school year, he dyed his hair black and wore it very long—shoulder length and more. Jet black hair had become a symbol for other young students in the junior high and high schools in the city.

An incident occurred in the high school next door, in which one of these young men, sitting in class, slit open veins in his arms and proceeded to bleed on the floor of the classroom. A young female teacher eventually noticed the pooling of blood under his desk and called the office for assistance. She was terribly 'freaked out' by the incident and the young man admitted to doing it for the sake of the notoriety it brought. He was given a school suspension, but little else was done.

Certainly, in retrospect, it is obvious that the situation was moving in a very dangerous direction. The young people involved in the witchcraft craze, were prepared to make very dangerous and difficult statements to attract the attention of peers and adults.

The following school year, I accompanied my wife to Germany, where she taught military dependents for the Canadian Department of Defense at one of their schools. I attended a German university and studied French in anticipation of eventually taking over a school with a French Immersion Program which was becoming very popular in Canada.

During the fall of that year, I was traumatized by the announcement, on world-wide radio, that two students from my previous school had committed suicide. I endured interviews of educators and parents during the following days, and determined that there was a great deal of inaccuracy and miscommunication in descriptions of what had actually happened. What was for sure was that the suicides were related to the witchcraft involvement of the young people.

The young boy that I had worked and counseled with for more than a year had killed himself. He had apparently knotted a rope around his neck and choked himself to death by tying the rope to the top part of a bunk bed and then hanging himself. On the following day, the other boy, a boy I had met through my administrative role in the school, but who at the time did not seem to have problems, also killed himself. He left a note in which he described a suicide pact with the other lad. They had agreed that if one of them were to die, the other would take his life also. Both boys were involved in the coven and both had long, dyed jet-black hair. Both had more or less dropped out of school prior to the deaths.

Even though I was removed from the situation, both literally and figuratively, the incident caused me a significant amount of personal and professional grief. Both boys were capable of so much, and yet, were unable to enjoy normal lives because of the early negative influences in their peer groups. How sad and tragic! It is absolutely essential that school administrators, counselors and teachers be aware of negative influences within a student body. While it is not always possible, obviously, to recognize how serious such influences might become, nevertheless, early awareness is tantamount to early warning. Appropriate steps to assist students to move beyond threatening circumstances are always possible.

Accidental

As principal of an urban junior high school, one often has to deal with issues that are tragic and sad. Early one Monday morning, I received a telephone call from the city police indicating that one of our grade 8 students had the evening before been found dead in his home and that preliminary investigations indicated that he had committed suicide. When the boy's name was stated, I was in shock. This young lad was one of our outstanding students; he was not a troubled boy; he was not having visible problems either with peers or with himself. He was doing well in school and had a wide circle of friends. The suicide just did not make any sense.

As in most situations involving the death of a student, an assembly was organized and school counselors and administrators informed the student body of the passing of their friend. In order to obviate against rumor and speculation, it was necessary to provide as much information as possible to the students to help them with their ability to grieve. Students who were seriously affected by the news were then scheduled for counseling with our talented and capable school counselors.

The funeral was planned by the family for the next Wednesday afternoon and school was cancelled for the afternoon in order that students could attend the funeral and grieve together with the family. Shortly before the funeral, one of the school counselors requested a meeting with me to discuss some disturbing information he was getting from students during counseling sessions. It seems that a story was circulating that the boy had not committed suicide, but that he had indeed died an accidental death. Inasmuch as the family and the police had not provided us with such information, we ignored the suggestion.

Several days after the very sad funeral, I was visited by a detective who came to the school to provide me with more information. The boy had indeed died as a result of an accident. Apparently, he was participating in a masturbatory practice when he died. He had tied a rope around his neck while in the shower, attached it to the top of the shower stall, and then physically choked himself while masturbating. This was the first incident of auto-erotic masturbation that I had encountered in my less-than-sheltered life. However, it was highly believable because a planned suicide for this student was so difficult to comprehend.

Unfortunately, the official version of the boy's death was and continues to be suicide. The family of course did not want to provide detail of the boy's death to the public and the police remained silent about their findings. As an administrator, I was upset to learn of this potentially tragic practice only after a student had died.

Automobile Accident

While principal of an international elementary-junior high school in the Kingdom of Saudi Arabia, the proximity to Mecca and the predominant Muslim population in the school combined to precipitate the death of one of our younger students.

An important facet of Islam is the pilgrimage to Mecca, at least one time in a Muslim's life. Many of the students in my school were in the Kingdom because their fathers, who were generally Pakistani, Indian or Filipino, had taken work in Saudi Arabia in order to facilitate the adherence to this important tenet of Islam. For youngsters to travel to Mecca with their families was a tremendous privilege. Young boys who performed the Hajj during the month of Ramadan or Umrah as the practice was called during the rest of the year, typically shaved their heads and dressed in white, just like their fathers.

During the school break that occurs because of holidays associated with the Eid, one of our grade 2 boys was privileged to accompany his father to Mecca. From our city, it was only about a four hour drive to the holy city. They proceeded to attend to the religious rituals associated with the Hajj, and after about four days, completed their pilgrimage and headed down the highway on holiday.

Not far from the shores of the Red Sea, and, consequently not far from Mecca, is an escarpment of considerable height. The boy and his family headed for a vacation spot in a city called Taif, high on the top of the escarpment. After a couple of days of rest and vacation, they headed down the escarpment to return home. The steepness of the highway and the relative disrepair of the family car contributed to the loss of brakes on the highway. The automobile left the highway at a high rate of speed, flew through the air and overturned several times before coming to a standstill. Miraculously, all family members survived, save one, the little boy in grade two. He was killed on impact.

The impact of this young boy's death on the faculty and students of the school was tragic. The announcement of his passing, which was brought into the school by a family friend, resulted in near mass hysteria—crying and public grieving. Adults, as well as children, were emotionally drained by the experience. Counseling, only available through the school counselor, was minimal and difficult. All schools should have practical plans in place to deal with such situations. Tragedy occurs every day and wherever large numbers of people gather on a daily basis, it is only a matter of time before it strikes someone within the population.

Nigerian Public Execution

One other experience which I feel a compulsion to describe was a public execution in Jos. (My experiences in Nigeria are described in more detail in Part 2 of this book.) On our arrival the first day in Kano, we had been taken to the home of a married couple who were working for an aid organization in Nigeria. As we stood in their front yard and talked, I heard frequent loud reports which seemed to be coming from not far away. Finally, I asked the hostess what that was. She said, "Oh, it is nothing. It is execution day today and they are shooting law breakers in the football stadium over there." I was flabbergasted by her response; a football stadium was just down the road from their house and was obviously filled with thousands of spectators. I had wrongfully assumed that they were there watching football (soccer). I made a vow at that moment to ensure that during my stay in Nigeria I would stay as far as possible away from any such public displays.

In Jos, which was significantly smaller in population and which was not a center for civil government, there seemed to be no executions—a circumstance for which I was thankful. However, near the end of our stay, information began to circulate around the university that there would be a public execution in Jos. It seems that a local young man had found an old rusty pistol in a local river. He had used this broken pistol to threaten a taxi driver and rob him of his money. Shortly he was captured by the police, languished in jail more than a year, and then, when finally he came before a judge, was convicted of armed robbery and attempted murder—with a rusty, inoperable pistol. He was sentenced to death by public execution and it would take place in Jos because that is where the offenses occurred.

We learned that the execution would be carried out on a Sunday afternoon in a long-abandoned race track. The track, which could still accommodate ten thousand people, was located half-way between the university and our home. As we traveled home from the university that afternoon, our van had to drive right past the site. I was startled by the large crowds of people who had gathered to observe the execution and marveled at the young boys carrying soft drinks in wooden boxes on their heads to sell to the spectators. We eventually were able to get past the track and arrived at home. Our houseboy had the television turned on and we discovered that there was local coverage of the execution. I opted to sit in front of the television and observe what happened.

Finally, several hours after the spectators had gathered, the police arrived in two vans. Ten uniformed officers carrying rifles by the handles on top of the weapon, (they looked like US M16A1 which were used by the US military in the Vietnam War) climbed out of the vehicles, formed up into formation, and at the command of an officer, ran into the arena. They halted about ten meters in front of a post which had been erected near the center of the arena. Immediately behind the post was a wall constructed of two rows of 50 gallon oil barrels, one on top of another. The barrels had been filled with sand and then stacked in two rows, one on top of the other.

The police arranged themselves in two rows, one row kneeling in front and the other standing upright behind. Moments later, a young man with his manacled hands behind his back entered the track. He was dressed all in white; his hair was meticulously coiffed in small beaded braids which covered his head. He was marched to the post and, with his hands cuffed behind him on either side of the post, he faced the soldiers. For a couple of minutes he sang a song in a tribal language, which my houseboy told me, was a traditional honor song for his family. Then, with no further ceremony, the commanding officer standing to the side of the armed soldiers gave the commands, "Ready, Aim, Fire!" The soldiers fired almost as one. It was obvious that some aimed at the youth's head, and the others aimed at his groin. He was immediately dead and the spectators howled and clapped. I was sickened and left the room.

Russian Deaths

Our home in Moscow (information on our experiences in Russia will be detailed in Part 2) was located just across a large and very busy thoroughfare called Leninsky Prospekt from the school where I was principal. One of the two buildings in which our school was situated was on the same side of the street as our apartment. Nevertheless, mornings I would drive my wife and children to the main building (a trip which took about fifteen minutes even though the apartment and school were only about five hundred meters apart...). Every day, usually before lunch time, I would walk back across Leninsky Prospekt to visit the pre-school building—housing the Reception (four year olds) and Kindergarten (five year olds) classes.

On one particular morning as we drove from our apartment through a passageway out onto Leninsky Prospekt, I saw a man lying on the sidewalk. As we got closer, it was apparent that it was a dead man; he was reasonably dressed in black leather coat, hat and with jeans and boots. I yelled at the kids to look down and continued driving slowly by. An ambulance had just arrived and two men were walking over to inspect the corpse. Because death and tragedy were never very far away in Moscow, we were not too surprised to see 'another' dead person. About two hours later that morning, as I walked back across the street to visit the 'little' school, I was quite taken aback to see that the body had not yet been removed. When I walked into the school, a little girl asked, "Sir, why is that man lying out by the road?"

Traffic in Moscow was seriously heavy and very dangerous. One morning, as I drove down the small road into the school, I noticed a little old 'babushka' crossing the street just ahead. She had obviously been shopping and was carrying a small metal pitcher of liquid. The driver in front of me did not notice her, and as she stepped in front of his car, he slammed into her. I will never forget the image of her flying into the air, her hair sticking out and the milk in her pitcher flying out in a stream above her. She flipped over in the air and landed on the windshield of the car which had hit her, breaking the window and becoming caught in the glass. By the time the driver ahead of me stopped, she had come to rest on the passenger side of the front seat. Unfortunately she was dead.

On another occasion, my wife and I had just left the school, driving to a meeting in another school located downtown. As we drove by Moscow State University which was only a short distance from our school, the traffic was very heavy and the going was slow. Suddenly, about thirty meters in front of us, a man, carrying a briefcase, darted out into the traffic with the intention of running through the traffic across the street. He had apparently already navigated the four lanes of traffic going the other direction, but sadly miscalculated on our side of the street. He jumped in front of a car that was traveling faster than was safe under the conditions. I knew that he was hit when the cars ahead of me hit their brakes and screeched to a stop. In the air high above our cars, the papers which had been in his briefcase drifted and flitted through the air. Traffic came to a standstill for about five minutes, and then began to crawl forward, four lanes melding into two as we passed the dead body. The man's head had been cracked open and blood covered the entire width of the street. Unfortunately, all vehicles had to drive through this pool of blood to continue on their way. I found it very difficult to concentrate in the meeting later that afternoon.

Natural Death in Saudi Arabia

One of my first administrative assignments after becoming an assistant superintendent, dealt with the death of one of our high school teachers. A young family man, he had gone to bed one evening and didn't wake up the next morning.

When the superintendent and I arrived at their home the first morning, the police were already there conducting an investigation to eliminate the possibility of homicide. The large number of policemen involved was a hint to the red tape we were about to encounter.

A death of a foreigner in Saudi Arabia was a difficult proposition. One couldn't just have the body embalmed and either buried or cremated, but in fact, it was necessary to attempt to have the body sent to the home country. Naturally there were many hoops through which we were compelled to jump and significant and numerous frustrations stood in our way. I accompanied the wife of the deceased to many civil government offices attempting to complete all investigations and obligations required to export the body. The amount of time required to accomplish these tasks was unbelievable—we spent many complete days wandering in and out of bureaucratic offices attempting to gain permission to send the body home. As I look back, I am amazed at the stamina and perseverance the young woman displayed in her pursuit of government permission; it was doubly difficult for her because the Saudi government is not set up to deal with a woman. On many occasions she was forced to wait literally hours for a short meeting or even completely ignored. In the meantime, the body of her husband was eventually embalmed and then kept in cold storage. Finally after many days, she was allowed to have her husband's corpse flown back to the United Kingdom for burial.

The world in which we live is cruel; all persons will eventually die. Unfortunately, death can often affect us in our work place, no matter where it is. It is essential that schools be prepared to deal with the loss of life which so often impacts students. Young people deserve to be educated in the potential of tragic loss of life and must be treated sensitively and tactfully when such incidents occur.

ASSAULT

Knife Incident

Shortly after I was appointed principal in my first junior high school, an interesting series of events occurred that opened my eyes to the potential dangers within schools. I was fairly 'wet behind the ears' as far as the principalship is concerned, and was not particularly ready for the event that took place that day.

It was a lovely warm day in May, literally days after I had been appointed principal when my predecessor left early for health reasons. I had already experienced several difficult situations in my introduction to the school, but the following stands out in my memory as exceptional.

I was wandering the hallways in the school, an older building with one 1920's section and one newer 1950's wing. As I meandered down the hallways of the older wing, picking up trash and disposing of it as I could, at the far end of the hall I saw an amazing sight. An older man, wearing a pair of Bermuda shorts, running shoes and nothing else, was pushing a grocery cart in front of him and was entering the hallway from the industrial arts room. Just as I noticed him, he immediately turned around and went back where he had come from, grocery cart and all. Now, I was a new principal, but was fairly certain that the situation was not normal. I proceeding down the hallway and followed the man into the shop, perhaps thirty seconds behind him. Inside the door, the students typically placed their books and possessions in "cubbies" (small cubicles or shelves), to have them out of the way during their industrial arts classes. I sought out the teacher who immediately pointed at another door and, quite excited, said, "He went that-a-way!" (Later, I was to discover that the man had been in the cubby area going through the student possessions when the teacher had spotted him and chased him out of the room into the hallway—right into my purvey.)

I immediately made a beeline back out into the hallway and ran down the corridor to the new wing, which was the direction the man would have had to go on the outside of the school. Sure enough, when I reached the main entrance door, I saw the man pushing the grocery cart ahead of him, running down to the main sidewalk in front of the school. I immediately ran outside to try to intercept him. The front of the school was higher than the street and sidewalk and I was therefore on a slight hill looking down on the man as he turned left, heading away from the school. I yelled something intelligent like, "Hold it! Where do you think you're going?" He turned, saw me coming, and stopped short. He put his hand into a paper bag in front of him in the cart and pulled out a very long and shiny hunting knife. He turned to me and said, "^%$##* you. I am going to take this knife and stick it up your *#% and twist it three times." Now I knew immediately that a serious situation was developing. I took in my surroundings and realized that if he were to come after me, his head, when he stepped over the small chain fence surrounding our property, would be below my feet and I, with a well-placed kick, could boot him in the head. I also realized that I could retreat into the school and call the police. As soon as I had the police on the line, literally in seconds, I informed them that this fellow was on the street, heading in the direction of the high school next door and that the situation was dangerous. I also telephoned the principal of the high school and warned him of the imminent danger, knowing that students often sat outside the school during their class breaks. I immediately went back out onto the street and observed police cars arriving from two directions. The bare-backed man immediately pulled his shiny knife and threatened the police. It took three policemen to subdue the fellow and handcuff him. Later, I learned that he had been released from a mental institution just a week earlier, and that the police had been watching for him because of his history.

Because schools are public buildings and most adults have spent significant time in them, the public feels comfortable and justified entering. Unfortunately, in this day and age, it is no longer possible for any and all persons to walk through the buildings. The safety and security of students must be foremost in our plans and public access should no longer be acceptable. It is also a concern that mentally deranged persons occasionally are present in public locations. Educators in schools are not instructed in ways to deal with these unfortunate persons.

Love and Hate

Unfortunately, fights are a reasonably common occurrence at schools. While educators generally abhor physical violence, it is not unusual to encounter students attempting to settle dispute through fisticuffs.

When I was a first-year teacher, I was teaching in a large high school in Hawaii. The school was unusual to my experience because all classrooms had doors opening to the out-of-doors, rather than into an enclosed hallway. Our school population consisted of two major groups: US military dependents, and locals. Animosities existed between the two groups, and there were further distinct groups within the two larger definitions. Within the military populations, divisions were obvious between officers' off spring and enlisted men's, as well as the, in those days, common divisions between blacks and whites. In the locals' group, cliques existed between surfers, Orientals and indigenous Hawaiians.

Needless to say, this convoluted circumstance led to many disagreements between students—and that without mentioning the natural tendencies in the 14 -19 age group to disagree over everything from politics to girlfriends and boyfriends.

On one particular day, as I was teaching English, I heard a fairly large commotion outside of my classroom. Being the curious type, I went to the doorway and looked out. There, on the campus grass just outside of my room, were two very large boys squaring off to fight. I knew they were going to fight because in those days the first thing they did was tear off their shirts—their own shirts. Randy, a very large Adonis-type black, stood a head taller than the local Hawaiian boy. Randy's body was perfectly toned and shaped muscle. The local boy was a head shorter, but had established himself around the school as a 'tough guy'. He had a cockspur beard (that is, the hairs growing at the bottom of his lower lip were about an inch long and curled) and several tattoos (before tattoos were all that popular among teenagers) on his well-proportioned body. They put up their fists and began to punch and jab—just like real boxers.

Teacher to the rescue! I immediately rushed out to separate the boys. Naively, I immediately positioned myself between the boys, who both towered more than a head above me. They hardly took notice of my presence. I yelled, "Stop fighting!" at the top of my voice—expecting results. All that happened was that I saw a shadow of doubt cross Randy's eyes which seemed to ask the question, "Shall I just kill this pipsqueak and get on with it, or what?" However, he seemed to pause slightly. Turning to the local boy, to yell at him, my head turned just in time to see "hate" coming directly at my face. (The local, it turned out, also had tattoos on the first joint of all of his fingers—'love' on one hand and 'hate' on the other.) I ducked my head just in time to only receive a glancing blow from the left hook along side my head. I thought he had torn my ear off. I saw stars and at the same time realized that his fist had glanced off the side of my head and hit my ear. To this day, I don't believe he was actually trying to hit me, but was throwing a wickedly wild punch at Randy. The fight ended immediately, as hitting a teacher was still taboo in that school in those days. I escorted the pugilists to the office and for the rest of the day nursed a very sore ear and a major headache—and had learned a very important lesson about breaking up fights.

Breaking up fights is not a lesson taught in teacher-preparation classes. Unfortunately, in our western society where violence is a method all too often used for settling differences, educators often find themselves in potentially dangerous situations. Perhaps some thought should be given to preparing school workers to know how to function in such situations with some possibility of obviating physical injury to themselves and the violence participants.

Hit the Principal

Students, like other members of society, come in all shapes, sizes and states of mind. Having called a student to the office to question him regarding an incident of fighting which had taken place the previous day, the principal began questioning the boy regarding his participation in the violence which had erupted in the school's hallway. The boy was, as they often tend to be, less than forthcoming about the incident, and in actuality, lied about his involvement. As the questioning became more and more pointed, the young man become more and more agitated. As it became obvious to him that the principal was in possession of evidence that directly linked him to the incident and described his participation in significant detail, the boy grew even less responsive to questioning and refused to speak. The principal picked up the telephone, purportedly to call the police, when the boy sprang out of his seat, vaulted over the principal's desk between them and slugged the principal in the nose. The principal grappled with the boy and wrestled him to the floor, hugging him to his body to keep him from throwing further punches. A secretary, having overheard the loud noises coming from the principal's office, summoned an assistant principal who entered the office and helped to restrain the student. Charges of assault were recommended by the police, but the principal refused to press charges and the student was only suspended from school for five days.

Teacher Hits Student

It was the last day of school in June and the summer holiday was about to begin. The French teacher, who was well-known in the school for his quick temper and his sarcastic treatment of students, had had an on-going verbal battle with a particular student for the entire school year. As the final bell sounded and students began to leave the school to head home for the holidays, this particular boy, walking through the hallway, made a snide and probably lewd remark about the teacher. The teacher, reacting to the student's facial expression and smirk, leapt across the hallway, grabbed the student and threw him up against the lockers. The student reacted violently and the teacher smashed him in the face with his fist. The student ran from the school shouting that "…he would sue the teacher and press charges against him for the attack." True to his word, the parents of the boy sued the teacher and the teacher was convicted of assault and paid a fine. In addition, the teacher who had worked in the school district for more than twenty years was temporarily removed from his teaching position.

Teacher Grabs Student

While teaching Grade 6, I had an experience that taught me one of the most valuable lessons I learned as a teacher. One of the bigger boys in my class was constantly attempting to make the day miserable. He was a clown, a disturber and a bully in class. He had not endeared himself to me, but, on the other hand, as is often the case, he was one of the students I most enjoyed. One day, during a lesson, the boy became very belligerent, and after the regular methods of discipline intervention had little effect on his behavior, I asked the boy to step out into the hallway to "cool down". My classroom had two doors, one at the front of the room and one at the back, both opening into the hallway. The boy immediately went out the back door and I headed out the front—just in time to see the boy running for the stairwell (we were on the second floor). I immediately ran after the lad and was right behind him when he pushed out of the outside door and ran across the playground. As a relatively young teacher, I was still active in sports and was able to catch the boy before he left the school ground. I grabbed him by the arm and stopped his flight. We turned around and proceeded back to the school. I walked him up the stairs to my classroom and prepared to speak to him about his behavior in class—after we had caught our breath. All of a sudden, he began to cuss at me and call me names. I am patient, but not that patient. I reached up and grabbed him behind the neck and gave, what I thought, was a gentle push. He fell to the floor and slid on his chest about ten feet toward the other end of the hallway. I was so mortified by his reaction, that I immediately became concerned that I had physically hurt him. I helped him to his feet, asked him to accompany me to the office, and essentially turned myself into the principal. I was convinced that my physical reaction to this boy would result in a suspension from teaching or even the loss of my job. To my surprise, the boy apologized profusely regarding his behavior and begged me not to tell his father. We discussed the situation and decided to move ahead; I only spoke to his parents about the incident several weeks later during parent/teacher interviews. They expressed understanding and I can count that exact incident as the one which taught me how NOT to deal with students. I never had occasion the rest of my career to grab another student in a threatening manner.

Parent Slaps Teacher

As principal of a fairly large school, Kindergarten through Grade 9, I often had occasion to meet with parents during times of stress. On one occasion, our secondary Science teacher was having a difficult time dealing with a mother who was unhappy with the report card grade her son had achieved. After they had met in his classroom, the male science teacher called the office and asked if he could bring the mother to the principal's office to continue their somewhat heated discussion. He was obviously feeling that they were not making much headway and felt that the principal could offer some support to the situation. Even though such meetings are generally arranged for in advance, it was obvious that someone needed to referee the discussion.

Moments later, the mother and Science teacher arrived in my office. It was obvious that they were not "seeing eye-to-eye". Their voices were very loud and they seemed to be talking past one another. After offering seats, I asked them to lower their volume and to speak one at a time. I turned to the mother and suggested that she begin the conversation by explaining the circumstances of her concerns. The Science teacher had taken a seat on a stool to the right-hand side of the parent and appeared to be waiting patiently for his turn to speak. The mother hardly uttered a word, when she suddenly stood, wound up and slapped the teacher openhandedly across the cheek. He was wearing glasses; they flew across the room and he lost his balance and nearly fell to the floor. A welt immediately began to grow on his cheek and he was visually surprised and physically hurt. He jumped off of the stool and headed for the outer office, yelling for the secretary to call the police. I had, in the meantime, jumped in between him and the mother and implored her to show decorum. The mother covered her face with her hands and began to sob.

Moments later the police arrived in my office and proceeded to take statements from the teacher and the mother. The teacher eventually dropped the assault charges he had been contemplating.

Parent Threatens Teacher

In the same school, on another occasion, a parent assaulted a Grade 6 teacher. It was during parent/teacher interviews; teachers were meeting parents according to a schedule in their respective classrooms. I was working in my office, content in the knowledge that interviews were moving forward smoothly and over 90% of our parents were meeting their teachers. All of a sudden, a young girl, Grade 6, came running into the office screaming that someone needed to rescue her teacher. I asked her the teacher's name and immediately ran out into the hallway in the direction of the classroom, shouting at the secretary to send our head custodian (a young, physically fit male) to the classroom. When I arrived at the classroom door, I found a male parent confronting the teacher and backing him up around the classroom. The teacher was trying to calm the father down, but having little success. The father swung at the teacher as I entered the room and hit him a glancing blow off of the shoulder. I yelled in my loudest and most indignant voice that he "…should back away!" To my surprise he did and looked up to see who was interfering with his assault. I identified myself as the principal and told him to leave the classroom with me. He followed me out of the classroom, and as the head custodian arrived, the father apologized to me and suggested that he had lost his temper because the teacher would not change the failing grade his daughter had received. The secretary had also called the school police liaison officer, who coincidently was in the school, and he also arrived. The father was taken away by the police officer; later it was reported to me that the father was high on drugs.

Hockey Player Threatens Student Body

While working as assistant principal in an alternate high school in Canada, the uniqueness of our program had an additional side effect--because students were able to work at their own speed in all courses, the local junior hockey team enrolled all of its players in our school. These young men were all players at the "Junior B" level of hockey, which meant that they had potential for playing in the major leagues. Many of our students eventually went on to become stars in the National Hockey League, players like Lanny McDonald (Calgary Flames), Brian Trottier (New York Islanders) and the Sutter twins, Rich and Ron who also had major league careers. Naturally, this type of talent, to be considered for the big leagues, required that the players, in addition to being highly talented, also had to be of considerable size to have a chance playing in the NHL. Because these young hockey players were often traveling, our school was the perfect place for them to finish their high school careers. This circumstance was usually of great interest and challenge to all concerned.

One Friday evening, with a school dance scheduled, I together with the other assistant principal and the principal had assumed our post at the entrance of the school to ensure that no one other than our students, or anyone high or drunk would be allowed into the dance. We had very few problems controlling the crowd that evening, and had welcomed more than 200 students into the school. All of a sudden, a car screeched to a stop in front of the school, and one of our hockey-player students emerged. (I will not divulge his name as he too went on to have a career in the NHL.) As he staggered and stumbled up the front steps to the school, it was obvious to all of us that he was either high or drunk. When he approached the principal, first in line at the door, he was greeted and then politely told that he could not come into the dance. He reacted in disbelief, and immediately began to argue. When it was suggested that he was indeed inebriated and could therefore not come in, he began arguing that he was not. His speech was so slurred and his demeanor so awkward—he began to drool down his front—that it was suggested that he leave the school grounds immediately or the police would be called. Instead of reacting positively to the sincere advice to leave before trouble began, he became even more irritated, loud and aggressive.

The entrance to the school was essentially a glassed in porch with double glass storm doors and glassed-in walls. This young man began to threaten all of us who were standing in front of him, impeding his access to the school. He stood about 6 foot 4 inches and probably weighed about 230 pounds—all solid muscle. The three administrators facing him averaged about 5 foot 9 inches in height and were definitely not muscular. As he became more and more agitated that he was not going to be allowed into the school, his speech became even more slurred, disjointed, threatening and abusive. All of a sudden he doubled up his fist and swung—at first it appeared to be at the principal's face—but then proved to be at the door jamb along side the principal's head. The entire glass porch, including all of the window walls shuddered; the boy hit the jamb a second blow. It was obvious that he was about to do serious damage. The other assistant principal headed down the hallway to the office to call the police the principal and I barred the young man's way. With a fury borne of frustration, he pushed the principal and me out of his way (not so hard for him to do) and barged into the school. He immediately headed in the direction of the gymnasium where already the dance had begun. We followed, yelling at him to stop and leave the school. Instead, he entered the gymnasium, went directly to the DJ's microphone which was located in the front of the gym, grabbed it and yelled into it,

"You are all a bunch of f***ing a******s and I will kill every one of you!" He said some other things as well, but then abruptly turned on his heel and headed back out the way he had come. Just as he ran out the entrance of the school, the police met him. They immediately grabbed him and, pushing him over to the lawn beside the front walkway, threw him to the ground. Just as they were putting handcuffs on him, his guardian (that is, the father of the home where he was staying) arrived and went up to speak to him. Many things were said, not the least of which was the admonition to not jeopardize his professional future by continuing to resist detainment.

On Monday, this hockey player appeared in the office to receive his punishment, five days' suspension from school, and to apologize to the administration. He was quite meek and humble during our meeting. He eventually went on to have a successful and eventful career in professional hockey.

Big Boy Assaults Little Boy

By far one of the more distasteful and horrifying assaults I was witness to occurred at an elementary school where I was assistant principal. This school had about 500 students in Kindergarten through Grade 6. As was common at most of our elementary schools, many events took place after school, ranging from homework help by teachers, to games clubs, and practices for sports teams. One afternoon, in late fall, several activities had been taking place and by five o'clock, most students had finished up and gone home. One of my assignments was to tour the school to make sure everyone had left and that there were no problems—no students without rides, students locked in rooms, students trying to get back into the school for whatever reasons, etc. As

I headed down the corridor where the Grade 5 and 6 classrooms were located, I heard a noise that sounded like a baby crying. Hurrying down the hallway, looking in each of the rooms and finding no one, I finally arrived at the outside entrance. There at the top of the steps was one of our Grade six boys kicking someone lying on the top step. As I rushed through the doors, the older boy kicked one final time at the little boy on the concrete, and then ran down the steps and into the street. I recognized the boy running away, but had to stop to see if I could help the lad on the steps. I turned him over and was shocked at what I saw—his face was a mish-mash of blood and cuts. His eyes were swollen shut and his nose was mashed and appeared broken. At least one of his front teeth was missing and the inside of his lower lip was lacerated and bleeding. Snot and saliva mixed generously with the blood pouring from his nose, mouth and other wounds. I held him in my arms and tried to comfort him. He was sobbing and struggling to get his breath. I picked the boy up, carried him inside the school entrance and tried to make him comfortable while I ran to the office to call an ambulance.

The young boy, only nine years of age, had been severely beaten by the Grade six boy who was already twelve years of age. Reason for the beating? The older boy claimed the nine year old had looked at him and laughed during the sports activity in the gymnasium.

Weapons at Dance

One has to wonder why school dances were tolerated in schools. Many of the most serious incidents of violence, suffering and stress were incidents that took place during school dances. Some of the incidents that occurred at dances have already been described, but the excitement never ends.

On one occasion, I recall supervising, as principal, a junior high school dance. The lighting at dances was generally very subdued and the crush of bodies significant. Some of the supervisors' major responsibilities were to ensure that students were not dancing too closely, that there were no drinks nor drugs consumed on the premises, that students were not fighting and that they did not sneak in and out of the dance.

As I was walking slowly through the crowd, joking and speaking with students, I noticed a group of boys on the opposite side of the dance floor who appeared to be up to no good. They seemed to be looking around surreptitiously, and were obviously handing something back and forth between them. I moved steadily across the room and used the poor lighting to disguise my approach. When I suddenly found myself among the boys, I discovered that they were passing knives, sickles and throwing stars back and forth. I insisted that four boys accompany me to the office, noticing that they had secreted the objects under their jackets. Imagine my surprise when I asked the boys to lay their 'items' on the table and three hunting knives, two sharp-bladed sickles (of martial arts style) and six razor sharp throwing stars were produced. Fortunately the boys seemed to be interested in sharing their possessions rather than having ideas of harming anyone with them. However, it did sober my thinking to realize that these items were carried into the dance without being noticed and that that would likely continue to be the case in the future—when the outcome would perhaps be more tragic.

Violence has been a significant characteristic of society throughout recorded history. This is not a valid excuse for violent displays, but a challenge to strive to eradicate violence in the lives of people. School, which many consider an accurate microcosm of the world, in general, is an appropriate location to teach the negativity of violence. However, it is essential that all members of society understand that eradication of violence is not the sole responsibility of school; it is necessary to understand that violence exists everywhere and to accept that there will be incidents of violence wherever people congregate. Schools must continue to teach youth that violence cannot be tolerated in a civilized world.

CHAPTER III

HUMOR

Shop Teacher Prank

All administrative incidents have not been associated with violence or tragedy. Occasionally situations develop in schools that are actually very humorous, but nevertheless require administrative intervention and decision. One such incident that immediately comes to mind involved a practical joke perpetrated by an industrial arts teacher on an acting school administrator. At the time this incident occurred, the principal of the school and both assistant principals (me included) were out of the school to attend an administrative conference. When this situation occurs, an acting principal is designated within the school and this person assumes the responsibilities and duties of the principal for a temporary period. Knowing that the regular administrative team would be out of the school, the shop teacher in question decided to "shock" the acting principal.

An emergency call, placed by a student in the shop class, was received in the office. "Please send someone to the shop immediately; there has been an accident and the teacher is bleeding. Hurry!" The acting principal ran full out the entire length of the school to get to the shop class from the administrative offices. Upon entering the classroom, he was confronted with a group of students ringed around a body on the floor. Pushing the students aside, the administrator was horrified to see the teacher, dressed in a white teaching smock, lying in a pool of blood with a wood chisel protruding from his chest. The administrator nearly fainted, but the laughing and snickering of students alerted him to the fact that all was not as it seemed.

The teacher rose slowly from the floor, smiled, and said, "Gotcha!" He had faked the accident with student collusion, using a broken chisel and faked blood to stage the accident. Everyone laughed long and loud at the circumstance and it was not long before the acting principal, likely out of relief, joined in. And then the ambulance arrived. Needless to say, the arrival of the ambulance and paramedics was a problem. There were reports to fill out and apologies to be made, and the incident had to be explained to the central administration. Funny? Yes. Appropriate? No. Memorable? Absolutely.

Fire Extinguisher Safety

A principal has to be concerned about safety in the school; for students and faculty. Naturally, a working relationship with the local fire department is warranted and, during my first year as principal, I attempted to establish just such a relationship. It was important to me to demonstrate to teachers that I was concerned about them and the students. On one occasion, I invited a fire fighter to come to a faculty meeting to instruct teachers on fire safety. The young man who arrived at the school was a relatively recent addition to the fire fighting business and it was obvious that he was quite nervous about speaking in front of so many teachers. Nevertheless, the teachers were polite and asked several questions, helping the fireman to feel at home. He had asked me to provide one of our fire extinguishers for demonstration purposes, and near the end of his presentation, he explained how extinguishers functioned. He suggested that the safety pin was very important and explained that the extinguisher would not put out a fire unless the pin was pulled. In order to demonstrate this safety feature, he turned to me and said, "I would like you to squeeze the handle as hard as you can; you will notice that you simply cannot turn the extinguisher on if the pin is present." He was holding the extinguisher nozzle in my general direction when I gripped the handle and gave it my best college try. I squeezed as hard as I could and the extinguisher, with a roar and a significant white cloud, immediately began to spray the area. The area was in fact me and I was immediately covered with white chemical! I, being a relatively quick study, released the handle of the extinguisher and covered my eyes. There was a long and deafening silence, and then the room erupted in laughter--I eventually joined in with the teachers and the hilarity lasted the better part of five minutes. I am sure that none of the teachers have ever forgotten that safety demonstration. And I know for sure that the fire fighter, who tried and tried, over the loud laughter, to apologize and to explain the malfunction, left the school vowing never to find himself in that type of position again. For several months after, whenever I encountered him or his fire-fighting colleagues, they referred to me as "chief" and had a good laugh.

Loss of Virginity

As I contemplate incidents in schools that were humorous, one of the funniest, in retrospect, was the day parents accused me as principal of the school for being responsible for their daughter's loss of her virginity. Obviously, it was not so funny at the time, but in thinking back, one can only laugh.

It is common practice to accept students into schools who are transferring from other schools—both from within a district, but also from out of city, state, province and/or country. A demanding responsibility is to assess transcripts from other organizations and determine in what classes and what grade level a transfer student might be accepted. On one particular occasion, bright and early on Monday morning a student appeared in my office requesting placement in our school. Even though the boy was slightly older than his previous school experience indicated, nevertheless, it was necessary to place him in Grade 9. He had several classes still necessary to complete before he would be accepted in our high school programs.

No problem. We placed Bill into a normal Grade 9 program and handed him a timetable. He was off to classes, and during the next five days, apart from some interesting first-impressions shared by some of his teachers, there didn't appear to be any significant issues.

The following Monday morning I was surprised to receive a surprise visit from the parents of one of our Grade 9 female students. She had accompanied her parents to my office. As they entered my workspace, it was obvious that the meeting was going to be emotional. The girl was sobbing, her eyes red and swollen, and so too, was her mother. She too had been crying and appeared to be very emotional. The father was angry; I did not know him well, but it is obvious when a parent is angry. I was of course interested in understanding what I could do to assist this family. In polite terms, I asked the parents what was wrong and how I could be of assistance. My surprise was total when the father began yelling at me that he would sue me and the school and the school district! Taken completely unaware, I had no idea what he was shouting about and I asked him to calm down—in order that we could talk. He responded that he would not calm down and that he was suing because I was responsible for the loss of his daughter's virginity!

I must say that that took me by surprise! I looked questionably around the room, hoping that more information was forthcoming. Eventually, the story unfolded. The new student, Bill, met their daughter during school the previous week. He was apparently quite attractive to her, and they set up a rendezvous on Friday evening to meet at her house while her parents were out. Nature took its course and the young people had sex. However, as fate would have it, the parents returned home early to discover the young people in a compromising position on the lounge in front of the television set. The father threw Bill out of the house and the parents elicited a confession from their daughter. Upon discovering that Bill was new to the city and the school, the parents decided that it was I who was to blame for the unfortunate situation that developed. Needless to say, the lawsuit never took place and the incident was soon forgotten. However, as I contemplate my experiences in school offices, this one tops my list of incidents which continue to make me laugh. (Of course, I felt sorry for the young lady and her family, but the accusation that I had had something to do with the loss of virginity continues to strike my funny bone.)

Teacher Masturbation

One of the stranger incidents that occurred during my first year as principal caught me totally unawares. I was principal of a junior high school and as such, found that I had very little time to sit in my office. Nevertheless, one day, after asking my secretary not to disturb me if at all possible, I was seated behind my desk working on a report when she came into the room. She looked a bit flustered and asked if she could disturb me. My policy was always that students, teachers and parents were priorities, in that order, and that written work could be done before and after school. "What is it?" I inquired. She said, "There is a young boy in the outer office who wants to report an incident in the boys' bathroom." "What? Oh, help. Well, send him in!" Seconds later a young, frightened looking boy came tentatively into my office. I could see immediately that he was very nervous and seemingly frightened. I told him to sit down and, after asking him his name and a bit about himself in an attempt to make him feel more secure, I asked, "What is wrong? What happened to you in the boys' room?" He began to stammer and squirm in his chair and looked like he wanted to leave. I coaxed him to calm down and talk to me. He finally muttered, "I saw Mr. Turner jerking off in the urinal." I stared at the boy for a couple of seconds and then said, "What did you see? Tell me slowly and clearly from the beginning." He continued to look very uncomfortable, but began to speak. "I was in my Science class and needed to go to the bathroom. I raised my hand and told the teacher. She told me to hurry and to come straight back to class. I ran down the hallway to the bathroom and pushed the door open. There, standing at the urinals, was Mr. Turner. He had his back to me, but was obviously pulling on his pecker. I didn't know what to do, and then, he looked over his shoulder and saw me standing there. He turned back to his business, did some adjusting and pulled up his zipper. I turned around and ran to the office." Well, it looked as if I was about to have another interesting day at school.

I sent the young lad back to class—by way of the boys' room—and asked my secretary to find Mr. Turner and ask him to come to my office. She looked up his teaching schedule, and because he was free that period, contacted him immediately. A few minutes later, Mr. Turner came into my office. He took a seat and asked, "What's happening?" It was my turn to squirm in my seat and then I swallowed and said, "Well, I just had a young fellow here telling me about an encounter he had with you in the boys' room. He suggested that you were masturbating into the urinal." Mr. Turner looked at me with a puzzled expression and then he began to laugh. He had a large voice and a tremendous laugh and it was infectious. Soon, we were both laughing and finally, I said, "So, tell me what is going on." Mr. Turner was in his final year of teaching and would soon retire. He said, "In all the years of my teaching, this is truly the first time I have been accused of masturbating in school!" He laughed. "It so happens that I am having some trouble with my prostate, and as a result of this I often have difficulty urinating. Whenever I have the urge to pee, I head into the bathroom and hope that I will be able to accomplish the task. Today, because it was in the middle of a class period and there were no students around, I went into the boys' bathroom on my floor instead of heading downstairs to the teachers' washroom. I was working hard, trying to urinate when I heard the door open behind me. I looked around and saw a young fellow standing there; I immediately zipped up and tried to look nonchalant. I guess he saw what he supposed was going on. Sorry." And he laughed some more. When we had both finished laughing, Mr. Turner asked what he should do. I told him to do nothing; I would call the boy back to the office and explain what it was he had seen. Minutes later, the boy was back in my office, standing before my desk. I said to him, "Sometimes when men get older, they have a hard time peeing because of a health problem; consequently they have to tug and shake a bit more than usual in order to pee. That is what you saw and Mr. Turner is quite embarrassed. I hope you can understand and that you won't be speaking about this incident to anyone else." The boy looked at me like I was telling a fib, and then said, "I won't tell anyone about it." He left the room, and it is my guess that he will only now begin to understand what was going on, as that incident occurred about twenty five years ago and he is about forty years old now.

Humor is one of the important factors which allow persons in the workplace to come together as a team. Educators who can laugh together have an excellent chance of being able to work together with effect. The capable administrator recognizes this as a characteristic of an effective teaching staff.

ILLEGAL

Crime in School

While principal of a junior high school which was located in the aging core of a small city, the school was burglarized on several occasions. This was weird, as there was rarely money or anything else of value in the school. However, upon finding little to steal, the burglars normally 'trashed' the office, resulting in significant difficulty and financial loss for the school. One year, after several break-ins, including a successful burglary of one school's office safe which netted the thieves more than seven thousand dollars (the proceeds of picture sale money), the police came up with a plan. In order to more effectively deal with the large number of break-ins in the school, the police initiated an interesting burglar alarm. Every evening before heading home, we were to dial a telephone number to a line in the police department and then place two large steel nuts on the main office telephone. (In those days, the telephone was activated when one took the handset off of the telephone cradle—that is, two small plastic projections which were held down when the handset was on the cradle, breaking the connection, popped up when the handset was picked up, thereby making the connection to the telephone line.) We placed the nuts over the projections before replacing the handset, thereby effectively keeping the telephone connection open, although with the handset in the cradle, it looked perfectly normal. The police receiver was placed on the desk right next to the radio dispatcher in the police station with the volume turned up very high. The dispatchers knew that no one was in the school and any conversations or unusual sounds heard would indicate that someone was in the office without permission. This method was highly successful, as, although I personally dealt with six or seven break-ins, none of the burglars ever figured out how we knew when they were in the school. Obviously whoever arrived in the school early in the morning or if I worked on the weekends, the 'burglar alarm' had to be dismantled and the connection with the line in the police station broken.

When the alarm was activated, the police would not enter the school building unless school authorities were there to unlock the doors. The principal's name was first on the list. Consequently, when dispatchers heard noises in the school, they did two things: they called the principal and said, "Would you come to the school immediately, we hear someone in there and need you to unlock the doors," and they called the police on patrol in the city so they could surround the school grounds before proceeding into the school.

I lived about a ten minute drive from the school and would therefore arrive quickly—no matter what time of the night it was. Because burglaries typically occur in the wee hours, I was usually in bed when the telephone call came. I would throw on some clothes and head to the school. The police asked me to approach the school without headlights on and to park near the property adjacent to the school. I would meet the police at the rear entrance of the school and, when they were ready, unlock the door. There were usually three or four officers, including a

K-9 handler and dog, who would enter the school and about four or five others who would be standing at locations around the school grounds.

Typically, the burglars were young men who thought burglarizing a school was a good way to earn a living and often, one of them would be a young lad who had actually attended the school at one time or another. Surprisingly, during the three years I was principal at that school, I never participated in catching a burglar who was a current student.

K-9 Policemen

About three o'clock one morning, I was called to attend my very first burglary. After unlocking the door, I stood aside in the parking lot as the policemen and their German shepherd entered the building. They remained in the building for more than a half hour, and finally, one of them came and asked me to enter the building. I went to the office and immediately recognized that desks and filing cabinets had been burgled, but the police had not found a culprit. The policemen asked me to accompany them through the school to see if I could ascertain where the 'bad guy' might be. The police dog by this time was done in; the school had two wings, one an old four story structure built in the early 1900's and the other a more modern four story which was added on in the 1950's. The floors, which didn't match up between the two wings, were highly polished and after traveling all of those floors, checking at classrooms and running up and down the many staircases, the dog was tired.

We waited a few minutes for the dog to recover and then, moved down the hallway away from the office and toward the shop and gymnasium areas. The dog obviously had a scent, but seemed to be having a difficult time pinpointing a location. When we went by the gymnasium, the dog seemed to want to enter and so we went in and turned on the lights. The gymnasium was in the old wing, and in addition to a full-sized gym floor, had a stage at one end. There were heavy curtains on the stage and I immediately noticed that one side of the drapes was hanging in a peculiar way. I looked more closely and was startled to see a pair of feet sticking out of the bottom of the curtain, which was wound up around a body. I called to the officer with the dog who was busy exploring the side storage rooms. They came immediately, and when I pointed out the feet, the policeman immediately led the dog to the stage, jumped up and approached the curtain. The dog was now going crazy, barking and jumping and pulling on its leash. The officer called out, "Hey, you son of a *****! Come out of there!" When there was no movement, the policeman, who was wearing typical heavy boots, began kicking the curtain. In just a couple of seconds, the curtain began unwinding and an obviously intoxicated man, about forty years old came stumbling out. The policeman wound up and kicked him directly in the butt, knocking him off of the stage onto the gymnasium floor. The dog was by now almost impossible to control, and the man was screaming, "Don't let him get me! Arrest me! I'm sorry!" and so on. Considering the circumstances, the situation was almost comical; the officer cuffed the man and that was the end of that burglary.

Six Burglars

One winter, on one of the coldest nights of the year—it was 42 degrees below zero—the telephone rang about three-thirty in the morning and I was asked to come to the school to allow entry. Upon arrival about fifteen minutes later, I noticed several police cruisers in the area, and when I approached the officer in the parking lot, he told me that they had heard several different voices in the school office. Four officers and the dog entered the school; I was asked to remain in the parking lot—and it was cold out there. As soon as they entered the school, a police 'paddy wagon' pulled into the parking lot and stopped near the back door. Within minutes, a policeman hauled out a young fellow, opened the back of the van, and pushed the cuffed youngster into the back. The boy was complaining about how tight the cuffs were and was generally belligerent to the policeman. A lot of profanity was going back and forth between the parties. Over the next several minutes, more young men were escorted out the door and dumped unceremoniously into the back of the van. Finally, there were six fellows in the van, and the officer in charge came out. He said to me, "We think there is one more burglar in the school, but have not yet found him. It is cold. Why don't you come in and see what has happened in the office while we look for the other fellow."

I went directly to the office and was confronted by a horrendous sight. All of the papers and contents of the filing cabinets were on the floor. The desks were emptied and all contents scattered everywhere. The computer monitors (we had only recently gotten our very first computers for the office) were broken and thrown on the floor. I entered my office, and discovered the same situation in there. The burglars had totally trashed my office. As I entered the room, I heard a slight noise coming from my desk. Moving cautiously and quietly toward the desk, I immediately perceived someone underneath it. I walked silently back out of the room and called quietly to the officer in the hallway. "I think your missing burglar is under my desk." He came quickly into the office with the police dog and entered into the back office. By the time I entered the room, the boy was standing against the wall with the dog standing in front of him. The dog had his paws on either side of the boy's head and was barking and slavering in his face. The boy was crying. Fortunately, the officer was keeping a tight grip on the dog's leash and not allowing him to bite the boy. By the time we got the seventh and last burglar out to the van, those already in there were yelling, complaining and hitting the side of the van. They were cold, but were showing off to each other by being difficult with the police. The dog handler walked up to the van, opened the door and said, "You b*******s had better be quiet or I will put my dog in the back with you!" You could have heard a pin drop.

Safe Safe?

Speaking of picture sales, it was not uncommon for schools to have break-ins during the picture sales' weeks. No matter what was done, the fact that the school was collecting picture money was always well known. When I was the assistant principal at a high school, I had an office which I was very proud of. It was located at the back of the main office, and was very large. In addition to my desk and files, a large conference table was located in the room because of its size. Of course, this was inconvenient when meetings were being held in the room because I could not work at my desk—however, this was a moot point because I most often had to be in whatever meetings were held there anyway. The inside walls of the school were made of cinder block, the large hollow bricks which were used in construction during the fifties and sixties. Our main office had a large walk-in safe, the door to which was a large, steel door with combination locks. We considered it to be the most secure safe in the school district and were not generally concerned about placing monies in the safe at night. Imagine my surprise when I arrived at work one morning to find cinder blocks strewn all across my office. We had had a visit from burglars during the night—they had known more than I did about the safe. By tearing down the cinder block wall in my office, they were able to gain access to the interior of the walk-in safe. We lost in excess of seven thousand dollars to those burglars; they had gained access to the school by breaking through a sky-light on the roof of the building. A new School Board policy was instituted shortly thereafter that disallowed any money over a $100.00 to be kept in a school overnight. That at least cut down the amount of money loss to burglars, but did not stop break-ins.

Blue Dye

One year we began to receive reports of thefts from lockers in the school. While it was not unusual for students to lose valuable items—there are always those who will steal—nevertheless, it was unusual for students to lose items from their lockers which were locked when they were closed. Unfortunately, thefts continued and students were losing significant amounts of money as well as tape players, radios and even expensive items of clothing. For several weeks we had such a rash of thefts from lockers, and even though we tried to monitor locker use (an almost impossible task because we had nearly seven hundred students and more than 800 lockers) and kept our ears to the ground trying to pick up clues, we eventually were forced to contact the city police and ask for advice. In the meeting the detective who met with us told us that it was nearly impossible to find the culprits unless we were to set a trap. We were not convinced that that would uncover the culprit either, but, as we had no other solutions, agreed to set a trap. The detective suggested we place an amount of money in a locker—the money to be marked with a special purple dye, which would immediately react with oils and moisture on the skin to mark the person or persons who handled it. We were not so sure, but we did it. After marking fifty dollars in bills with the purple dye, we placed the money in an empty locker and began, what we thought, would be a long wait. Were we ever surprised!

The very next morning, one of my advisees (students in my advisor group) called in and said that he would not be in to school—he was sick. On checking later with his mother, a routine call from a secretary regarding absent students, we were told that he was not sick. We became suspicious, checked the locker with the money, and discovered that it was missing! Later that afternoon, my advisee came into school, accompanied by his mother. His hands and clothes were covered with the purple dye! What a success! He told us that he had found a passkey to the school-issued lockers and that he would wait until later on in the evening, and would then search lockers for items he wanted. Because of the size of the school, he was able to foresee where the custodians would be working and thereby was able to dodge them. We were compelled to report him to the police, but suggested to them that, if he would return the money and valuables, we would appreciate only a suspended sentence.

Teachers Steal Too

Students were not the only thieves in the schools. On one occasion, because we required teachers to contribute to the coffee fund by placing money in a coffee can we kept in the teachers' lounge, it became obvious over a time that the money was going missing. Although teachers were placing money in the can, there was never enough money to buy new stocks of coffee, sugar and creamer when the current stocks ran out. As I pondered the implications, it came clear that someone was pilfering the money. I couldn't be sure if it were a teacher, a student who was sneaking into the lounge, or a custodian who was the thief. But I was determined to find out. Once again, I had to figure a means by which I could discover who the thief was. I couldn't really use the purple dye, as many persons handled the money and I couldn't be sure that the thief would be one of them. Finally, I decided to set up a camera, and see if I could determine who would take our coffee funds. In those days, the cameras were Beta cameras, transferring the imagery to Beta tapes contained in the camera. Of course, because of these large cassettes, the camera was very large. How to disguise it? Eventually, I simply placed a large cardboard box on the window sill and left it there, empty, for a few days. As is normally the case in a teachers' lounge, no one really noticed the box, and if they did, they left it where it lay as no one was sure whose it was or what its purpose was. When I finally placed the camera in the box, directed toward the coffee can through a small hole in the side, I was sure no one would notice. Each evening for nearly a week, I would turn on the camera before I left the school in the evening and just let it run until the tape was full. It was less than a week later, when, viewing the tape on fast forward I was able to notice someone in the film. When I slowed it up, I was shocked to discover that our thief was one of our teachers! When I called the teacher into the office and confronted him, he denied the accusation, but eventually confessed that he was taking the money after I showed him the film.

Thievery, like violence, seems to be a negative characteristic of the human make-up and therefore one which we encounter frequently in schools. Unfortunately, no matter where people gather, whether in school, the work-place or in social situations, some persons will steal. In schools, it is important to teach young people why stealing is bad and to help them protect themselves against personal loss. However, theft will likely always be with us.

DRUGS

Desks

The years during which I worked in schools coincided with years of serious drug abuse among young people. In every school I worked, drugs were in use—even though not necessarily apparent. Because I worked in Hawaii during the height of the Vietnam War and Honolulu was a popular destination for rest and recuperation for soldiers, drugs of every type were available to students. In Hawaii, one of the teacher tasks was to clean the room after school each day. Students were assigned to clean out desks, mop the floors and clean the blackboards. Several times my students would call me to inspect desks in which the remnants of glue sniffing had been hidden. Plastic baggies with the residue from glue were stuffed into the backs of desks. One would ask how a student could possible sniff glue during school time… the answer was that my classes always had more than 40 students in them. In a classroom built to accommodate 25 students, it is not hard to lose track of students. During the lunch hours, it was not uncommon to smell the distinctive aroma of marijuana as one walked down the open hallways. Students would congregate just off the school property and smoke drifted into the school yard.

Parking Lot Busts

While working as an assistant principal in a high school in Canada, I would frequently observe students entering cars in the parking lot, which was located behind the school, rolling up all the windows and smoking. Of course, it was not always cigarettes being smoked. I, on several occasions, interrupted the smoking parties and invited the students into the office for discipline. The normal punishment for smoking drugs was suspension from school. Students were not allowed back in until their parents came and helped us work out an agreement which had a serious drug clause, indicating that further drug use would result in expulsion. I rarely saw a student expelled for drug abuse.

Hash Knives

As principal of a junior high, I can remember a highly indignant mother coming into the school one day to complain because students had ruined her silverware. Her daughter apparently had thrown a party at her house and the mother was angered to find that many of the table knives had been burned on the stove. She thought that this had been a malicious act, and wanted me to help her find the vandals. She was horrified when I explained to her that the knives had been used to burn hash in order for students to smoke it. I would not have liked to been in her daughter's shoes when she arrived home from school that afternoon.

The use of drugs during the school day, while disturbing when it occurred, nevertheless was infrequent. That is, with the exception of marijuana use in high school, often difficult to detect, drug use was almost never recognized as a hindrance to learning. It is without doubt that many high school students used drugs, but unlike alcohol use, would not typically advertise their use during school time. In speaking with teachers of option classes, such as music or art, it is clear that students would often smoke a joint before coming to class. But for the most part, they maintained a low profile and consequently were rarely reported.

CHAPTER VI

ALCOHOL

Martini Lunch

Oddly enough, it was the abusers of alcohol who were more often reported in school. Probably because the effects of alcohol abuse are much more difficult to disguise, students were suspended for drinking far more often than for drug use.

I recall an incident where a young female student arrived to class after lunch and, after sitting down at a desk in the classroom, vomited all over the desk, the floor and herself. I was in the office and received an urgent call over the intercom from the teacher, asking that I come immediately to the classroom. When I arrived, the teacher and the rest of her students were standing in the hallway, most deploring the stench emanating from the open door. I went in to the room and found the girl, fast asleep, lying in her vomit on the desktop. As distasteful as the situation was, I shook the girl by the shoulder until she was conscious, and then assisted her to stand and accompanied her to the office. (In the meantime, the teacher called a custodian who came to the classroom, threw sawdust on the desk and the floor, cleaned up the mess and school went on as usual.) Meanwhile, in the office, I called the girl's mother and, after explaining what had happened, asked her to come to the office to pick up the student and take her home. The mother was indignant and suggested that it was the duty of the school and its staff to take care of the girl, because, after all, it was during school time! After explaining to her that my only recourse was to call the police and have the girl arrested for public drunkenness, she agreed to come and take her home. When she arrived, she continued to chastise me for being pitiless and mean and for shirking my duty as a school administrator when I would not take care of the girl for the afternoon. As the mother helped the girl to the door, I informed her that she should keep the young lady home for the next three school days as she was suspended for abusing alcohol at school. The woman called me a series of picturesque names as she escorted her daughter out of the school.

I experienced incidents of alcohol abuse in elementary school, junior high school and senior high school. The deplorable fact was that young people seemed to have unfettered access to 'booze' in their homes. And, it seemed that students believed it would somehow enhance their image among their peers if they defied authority, and imbibed before coming to school. Unfortunately, the opposite was true. Students who would ignore other types of misbehavior—fighting, lying, cheating, drug use, and even alcohol abuse at other school functions—seemed to attach a stigma to alcohol users who came to school under the influence and the abusers usually experienced significant socialization issues.

Drunk at the Dance

One Friday evening, while supervising a dance in the junior high gym, it became very obvious that a girl was having difficulty walking and remaining upright. I and a supervising teacher escorted the girl to the office and sat her down in a chair. She was so highly intoxicated that she was unable to speak coherently. As was so often the case, she became ill and threw up her malodorous supper onto the carpeted floor. The teacher went to find the appropriate materials for cleaning up the vomit and I began trying to locate the girl's parents on the telephone. Unfortunately, about that time, she lost control of her bodily functions and made a further mess in her trousers. What a horrible situation! I was fortunately able to reach her father and he agreed to come to my office and pick the young lady up to take her home. The cleanup accomplished, I remained with the girl in my office awaiting her father. About this time she began to cry and sob—anticipating, I am sure, the trouble which awaited her at home. Her embarrassed father arrived, helped her to her feet, and as she stumbled out the door, she said, "Mr. Bowen, you're not going to punish me, are you? This is the first time I have done anything bad." Oh, how I loved the naiveté of youth!

Alcohol is a serious problem for young people. Just as with adults, many of the tragic and lamentable incidents which occur in life are a direct result of alcohol consumption. Schools are aware of this and attempt to stem the abuse of alcohol with severe punishments—usually suspension from classes. However, schools are far less effective in their attempts to abolish alcohol use than are parents. Because the use of alcohol for adults is acceptable in our society, however, young people tolerate punishments, but do not seem to alter behaviors in this regard.

AWKWARD AND DIFFICULT

Vandalism

It is not uncommon to have many students transfer in and out of a school during the school year. Occasionally, the reasons for the transfer are not obvious. During my second year as principal of a junior high school, I processed the transcript for a Grade 9 boy, who transferred into my school near the end of October. He was transferring from a relatively large school in Vancouver, British Columbia; his records seemed normal. When he arrived at school, he turned out to be a tall--significantly over six feet--lanky boy with a definite chip on his shoulder. He made it clear from the outset that he was not happy about the transfer to our school, nor was he about to take much direction from the administration or teaching staff. He was his own man... It didn't take long to realize that there were going to be some problems. He was fifteen, going on twenty-five, and wished to establish himself socially. He immediately began to have problems with several of his teachers, and within the first week of his attendance, visited the office on several occasions to discuss his behavior.

Near the end of his second week in school, I was called to the boys' locker room by his physical education teacher, to observe an act of vandalism. When I arrived, everyone was standing around waiting to see what would happen. The teacher was fairly animated—irate and began to yell about the destructiveness demonstrated by the new boy. He, on the other hand, was playing the role of tough guy for everyone present. Once I was able to get everyone settled down, the teacher pointed out to me that the thermostat which controlled the heat levels in the gymnasium had been broken from the wall. The thermostat was located about five feet from the floor, and yet, it had been obviously smashed. Upon questioning, the new boy admitted to breaking the thermostat by applying a well-aimed roundhouse karate kick to the instrument. He was wearing very large and heavy boots, which at the time were the rage, and it was quite amazing to realize that he had been able to kick that high.

I returned with the new boy to the office and called his father. His father answered the telephone, and was not pleased when I informed him that he would need to visit the school immediately, or his son would be suspended. About an hour later, a terribly loud racket came from the front of the school; I looked out of my office window just in time to see a rather large, hairy individual, complete in a Hell's Angel leather jacket, ride forcibly up the front sidewalk to the front steps of the school on a large and noisy Harley Davidson motorcycle. He dismounted and ran up the steps to the front doors of the school. I headed out into the hallway which was full of junior high school bodies (it was precisely during a class break), just in time to hear, shouted at the top of his lungs, the father shout, "Where in the f*** is the principal's office?" Needless to say, I immediately cornered the man, who had somehow quieted the masses of students walking through the hallway, and invited him to accompany me into the office.

The conversation began rather loudly, and I eventually lost my patience and yelled back at the man. Once I had raised my voice, he seemed to take notice of me, and calmed down. I explained what had happened in the locker room, and explained that his son would have to pay the repair costs and "clean up" his act, or he would not be allowed to continue to attend school. The father, looked at me, looked at his son, and then, with tears in his eyes, apologized. He then explained that he had brought his son from a difficult situation in Vancouver—the boy had had several problems with schools and the police—and that he was hoping he would have a new start in our school. The conversation ended amicably enough, the costs were covered and the new boy was admonished to not create any more problems. I believe the father's exact words were, "You quit causing problems or I will kick your a**!"

Later, I learned that the father was one of the leaders of the local chapter of Hell's Angels and that he was deeply involved in the local drug scene. This did not stop him, however, from coming to all PTA meetings or from calling me on frequent occasions to invite me to 'parties'. During that particular time, we were having some problems with the institution of "sex education" in our school, and there was a very vocal clique of parents who made all public meetings nearly unbearable. I will never forget how Flic (for this was his name), stood up in the audience and told those parents, "… to pull their heads out of their a***s, and to quit being a problem for the rest of the students." It was truly an interesting meeting.

Unfortunately, Flic and his son did not last long in our community. An imminent drug bust drove them out of the city and they were not heard from again.

Neighborhood Cleanup

Not all circumstances administrators must deal with are crime, violence, alcohol or drug related. On a daily basis, situations occur which require an administrator's involvement which can best be described as "difficult". Because all people in North America have gone to school, many truly believe that they are school experts, that is, they know best how to deal with any and all situations in schools. Over many years, there was very little respect for the teachers and administrators in schools, and because of sayings like: "Those who can, do; those who can't, teach." (Attributed perhaps to G. B. Shaw), many people believe that those persons involved in education are somehow lesser versions of successful people. Unfortunately, this narrow view of education and educators often led to awkward and difficult situations.

While serving as the newly-appointed principal of a medium-sized junior high school, I was very concerned about the difficulties associated with neighbors—those people who were unfortunate or fortunate enough to have homes located close to our school. Teen-agers typically paid little attention to concerns of homeowners; trash, trespassing, and occasionally vandalism were the scourge of such neighborhoods. It was one of my concerns that all students treat the neighbors with respect and attention. With this in mind, I organized periodic "clean-up" days during which students would roam the neighborhood on every side of the school for about a city block and pick up trash and garbage from lawns. During the severe winters, I instigated "snow-shoveling" brigades who would shovel the snow from neighbors' sidewalks, in particularly those of elderly neighbors. Nevertheless, even with these types of attempts to appease those living near the school, I learned that neighbors were rarely happy.

Before I had set up a neighborhood clean-up program, I was in the outer office one day speaking with the secretaries, when a gentleman entered the office carrying a large, black, plastic bag. As the receptionist asked how she could help him, he said, in a voice full of sneering derision, "This is the garbage from your school which I picked up off my lawn this afternoon; I want to know what you are going to do about it." His demeanor was so negative and demeaning that I could not help myself; I strode through the gate to the front office, took the garbage from the man, and saying something like, "We are trying to deal with more than seven hundred teenagers in this school, and believe me, we have far worse problems than this small bag of garbage to deal with." Upon saying that, I swung the garbage bag over my shoulder and slammed it into the small trash can standing by the front counter. Naturally, because the trash can was small and the bag was bigger, not to mention the fact that it was traveling at half the speed of light, the bag hit the edge of the can, broke open and the contents flew all over the office. Everyone, secretaries, neighbor and I included, stood there in stunned silence. Then, the tension broken, we began to laugh. The neighbor joined in the laughter and, when we finally were able to settle down, I invited him into my office for a talk. The "clean-up" program described above was the result. I had always felt that I reacted immaturely to his complaint, but it did indeed work out.

Christmas Concert Meltdown

Extra-curricular events were naturally the responsibility of the principal and staff. Ensuring that teen-agers would act responsibly and that they would always represent our school in positive ways were perhaps examples of wishful thinking, but were nevertheless important concerns for the administration. Interestingly, it was not always students who let us down. One of the highlights of the first semester of each year occurred shortly before the Christmas Holidays—the Christmas Concert. Students in our music programs worked hard during the first four months of the school year to prepare for their exposure to the public. Inasmuch as music students were participating in music for school credits, it was always assumed that they would work hard to prepare themselves. Our music teachers were well-trained and very professional. It was always appreciated by the administration and staff when the students performed for parents, families and the public as it was a clear demonstration of classroom learning. Of course, there was a great deal of pressure on the music teachers, because only they, with perhaps the exception of physical education teachers, were required to demonstrate their capabilities and teaching success publically.

In elementary school programs, 'goof-ups' are not uncommon, and in fact, are what make the programs more appealing and endearing to the audiences. Everyone loves to laugh at the little ones who can't remember lines, forget where to go, wave at parents in the audience and even pick their noses. But by the time students are in junior high school, it is assumed that the concerts will be more professional and polished. In my second year as principal, the long-awaited and much practiced Christmas concert was well-attended. The auditorium was absolutely full—standing room only. A variety of musical pieces by the choir and smaller instrumental groups had been performed and applauded. Our band director, who had taught Music in our school system for many years, took the podium to direct the band in the final number on the program. As he waved his arms to indicate that the musicians should begin, there was a feeble and squeaky chaos of sound—no one seemed to know what to do. The teacher rapped his baton on the metal music stand in front of him demanding attention and quiet, and began again. Once again the band members were unable to begin, except for a few awkward noises. This time, the director stood embarrassed for a few moments, and then, in a gesture I had not before seen, stomped off the stage and out the door of the auditorium. Of course, it fell on my shoulders as principal, to end the concert and send everyone on their way with wishes for an enjoyable holiday. As the people moved toward the doors, many parents made their way up to me to complain about the end of the concert. Inasmuch as I had no idea what the problem was, I could only commiserate with them and their children and express my hopes that such a thing would not occur again. How embarrassing for the students, the reputation of the school and for me, personally, as principal. The teacher, who also taught Math, was relieved of his music teaching assignment the following Monday and remained on staff for the next several years as a math teacher.

Nervous Breakdown

During my first full year as principal, a teacher came to me one day and asked if she could speak to me about an issue that was very sensitive and confidential. We made an appointment after school that afternoon; later she came into my office and sat down. Immediately she began to cry. I waited for her to gather herself and eventually she told me the following. Her husband, a good man, came from a family in which the males were afflicted with Alzheimer's Syndrome. Even though he was fairly young, at that time in his early forties, his father and then his brother had suffered the onset of the disease early in their lives, and both had died from it before they reached fifty years. The story was heart-wrenching, and yet, I was surprised she was telling me this. When I asked her why, she told me that her husband had, just that morning, taken the milk carton out of the refrigerator to put milk in his coffee, forgotten what he was doing with the milk and dropped it on the floor. She was convinced that this was an indication that he too would soon suffer from Alzheimer's. After doing my best to console her by suggesting that it was perhaps only a fluke, she agreed, but suggested that I should know of the situation in case it became an issue during the school year. I thanked her and that was the end of the conversation at that time.

Several weeks later, my secretary came into my office abruptly one morning and told me that students in that particular teacher's classroom had called in on the intercom and asked that someone come to help their teacher. Jumping from my desk, I ran through the hallway, down the stairs to her classroom. I opened the door to absolute silence, a situation not that common in a Grade eight classroom. Standing in the front of classroom was the teacher, her hands covering her face and her tears. She was sobbing quietly and not moving. The students were dumbfounded and obviously not sure what to do. I went to the teacher, put my hands on her shoulders and spoke to her. "Mary, what is wrong?" There was absolutely no response. I thought it best to attempt to get her to leave the classroom with me and put one arm around her waist to assist her. There was no response; her feet seemed to be frozen to the floor. She had not yet acknowledged my presence, but had begun to cry aloud. I again spoke to her, "Mary, it is Fred. Please come with me. I want to help you." She looked up into my face and recognized me. She turned into me and began to cry on my chest. I held my arms around her and let her cry. The students continued to look with stunned expressions—none of them said a word. Finally, after nearly five minutes, I was able to slowly walk Mary to the door of the classroom. I grabbed a chair and placed it in the hallway and sat her down. I stepped back into the room, called the office on the intercom and asked for the assistant principal to come down. Fortunately, he had been told of my rush from the office and came down the stairs at that moment. Together we picked Mary up and moved her up the stair to my office. She was inconsolable, so we arranged for one of the staff to take her to the hospital. Later, I learned that her husband had left home the previous afternoon for a walk and that he had been missing for most of the day. Even though he had grown up in the city, he had been totally confused and, eventually, was picked up by the police who had brought him home. Mary went on leave and, after her husband died in the early spring, did not return to teaching for more than a year.

Inappropriate Relationship

My wife was hired by the Canadian Department of Defense to work in their high school for dependents in Lahr, Germany. Although I was not hired, nevertheless, I would accompany her as a dependent to Lahr. Inasmuch as I had been a junior high school principal for more than three years, I applied to our school board in Alberta for a leave of absence. Our board was willing to give me a two-year leave which was consistent with the length of my wife's contract with the Department of Defense. In addition, I applied to the board for a stipend which would allow me to attend university while living in Germany, using the rationale that, in case I should become principal of one of our schools which sponsored a French Immersion program, it would be good to have a reasonable knowledge of French. At the time, our school district had few administrators who were fluent in the French Language. For more than a year, I was able to attend French classes at a German university in the city of Freiburg im Schwarzwald.

Upon returning to Canada after two years in Europe, I was assigned as principal in a school with multiple programs. Because of my previous teaching and administrative experiences in elementary, junior and senior high, this appointment was logical—plus this school had a French Immersion program. The school was a serious challenge, because, in addition to the combined grades and a French Immersion program, the school also had a program for the severely handicapped and was a community school. Each of these significant programs provided distinct and serious challenges for the administration of the school.

Upon arrival during the summer of 1991, a teacher who had worked for me in my previous junior high school assignment contacted me and asked if he could join me in the new school. He was flattering in his description of the reasons he wished to join me there, and, that notwithstanding, he had been one of the finer, young, enthusiastic teachers I had worked with. Naturally, I was pleased that he wished to join me in the new school and believed that he would bring significant strength to the teaching staff.

As that school year progressed, the addition of this particular young teacher proved to be felicitous as he provided energy, charisma and support to students and teachers alike. In addition to his regular teaching duties, he was a coach, participated in all staff activities and was the advisor for the students' council. His contributions to the school were exceedingly appreciated by me.

It came to my attention that this young man had been frequently seen outside of school in the company of a student. Shortly thereafter, I called the teacher into my office and asked him pointblank if there was any type of relationship between him and the student. He appeared shocked and vowed emotionally that there was no such thing. We discussed the difficulties which could arise because of appearances and he agreed that he would ensure that such situations would not happen again.

In the weeks following, I spoke with the young teacher on several other occasions and he assured me that he had acted on the discussion we had had and that no further situations had developed. Several months later, I received a telephone call from the superintendent of schools asking me about the young man and his relationship with a student. I detailed to him all of the events that had occurred in the previous months and told him that I was reasonably certain that nothing untoward was happening. However, I suggested that should he wish to investigate the matter further, I would be as helpful as possible.

Approximately a month later, the superintendent called me and asked me to arrange a meeting with the teacher after school in my office. I set up the meeting. That afternoon, after the teacher had settled in my office, there was a knock on the door and the superintendent, accompanied by a man in a business suit, entered the office. With no further ado, the detective, then that was how he identified himself, accused the young man of having an inappropriate relationship with a minor, read him his rights under the law and placed handcuffs on him! I was devastated! That was the last time I saw this teacher as he was placed in jail and eventually convicted. He was sent to prison; his teaching certificate was revoked. Several months later he called me from prison to tell me where he was and that he was serving time. He claimed innocence and never apologized for the lying and malfeasance he had displayed to me.

This was one of the more difficult and defining moments of my entire educational career. While it has always been my philosophy that teachers are professionals and therefore qualified to function independently of me as an administrator, nevertheless, in later years, I occasionally tended to become somewhat more skeptical of a teacher's professional veracity. While I have never lost my respect and admiration for teachers, I have learned to check and double-check that all is well. Teachers too are fallible and sometimes need support in their personal lives as well as in the classroom.

Leadership

The nearly twenty-five years that I worked in public school systems taught me a great deal—in particular during the fifteen years I was a school administrator. In the 1970's, when I was first appointed as an assistant principal, my qualifications for an administrator position were nearly non-existent. I had had the good fortune to teach in high schools and elementary schools, and had therefore significant opportunity to observe closely both ends of the public education continuum. However, during those years I had never taken a class in administration, never worked in a school office nor even functioned as an acting administrator. My exposure to school management was confined to those rare opportunities I had to observe administrators in action. Nevertheless, my exuberance in my aspiration to become an administrator outweighed all else and I was eventually able to convince my superiors that I was a capable candidate.

As you have seen in the foregoing accumulation of school incidents, I collected a wide variety of experiences which helped to forge my thinking as an administrator. Initially, during my early years as a teacher, I assumed the principal of a school was the leader of the teachers, who, in his spare time, managed the physical operation of the school. However, so many unusual events occur daily in the life of a school, the role of an administrator was profoundly different than what I had imagined.

So, what did leadership mean? As I began collecting experiences with teachers, I gradually changed my thinking from the simplistic concept of an officer propelling men into battle by waving a sword over his head and leading the charge, to the more realistic acceptance of a leader working closely together with persons he knew personally and whom he respected to accomplish common goals—in our case, the education of children.

How does one engender relationships with teachers to accomplish such a worthy goal? Teachers come in all shapes and sizes; they have varying backgrounds, education, personalities, skills and talents, beliefs and prejudices. They look at the world differently and relate to their position in that world in ways too numerous and varied for any one person to recognize and understand. However, the effective administrator must work closely and effectively with all. It is not enough to work closely with the small percentage of outstanding teachers, but equally as necessary to work with the majority of teachers who are average--and, unfortunately, those below average.

As I contemplated my experiences as an administrator, I came gradually to realize that all effective teachers have a common goal—to help all young people learn. Although the methodologies, philosophies, successes and failures were different for everyone, nevertheless, the goal was ultimately the same. Recognizing, respecting and accepting teacher differences leads to effective administration. Teachers enjoy working with administrators who respect their successes, no matter how they reach them, and who accept that their failures can be improved upon. As long as the administrator is able to keep this goal in mind--we are all there to assist young people to learn--working with such a variety of professionals effectively is possible. Good schools and effective education are the results.

The unusual experiences one gathers while working as a school administrator, whether they be dealing with death, violence and unlawful acts, or humorous or awkward incidents, forge the links in the chain between the teaching faculty and the administration. The more effectively the administrator is able to deal with a long and varied gamut of incidents, the easier it is to establish rapport and support among the teaching staff. The school community and the overall effectiveness of the education provided there are significantly strengthened when such incidents are appropriately administered.

PART 2

INTERNATIONAL EDUCATION – NIGERIA

During more than fifteen years as a public school administrator, I was able to accumulate a large number of experiences that enhanced my effectiveness as a school leader. Public education is a challenging and potentially fulfilling venue for an administrator's career; however, through a series of circumstances and opportunities, I was able to add another source of experiences to my repertoire as a school administrator—international education.

Nigerian Administrative Experience

By virtue of my experience as a visiting professor of education at the University of Lethbridge, in my second year as principal I was invited by the university to participate in a professor exchange with the University of Jos in Nigeria. The two month opportunity would occur in the summer and I would therefore not need any type of leave from the public school system. I was invited to the university for a meeting where I met the others, three education professors, who would also participate in the program. We learned that two of our colleagues would be bringing a child each with them to Nigeria—a boy in his twenties, and a high school-aged girl. During the meeting, in order to facilitate correspondence and to make final decisions, a vote was taken and I became the ad hoc leader of our group—because of my experience as a school administrator.

Immediately after the close of school for the summer, we headed for Nigeria. The trip was eventful and quite nerve wracking, as we were not sure what type of welcome awaited us in Nigeria. Because the exchange had been put together quite quickly, right up to the day of departure we were not completely sure where we were going. Nevertheless, we eventually arrived at the airport in Kano, northern Nigeria.

As I walked down the steps from the airplane onto the tarmac, I had only taken two or three steps when I heard, "Fred Bowen! What are you doing here?" How was this possible—recognized by someone at the most remote place I had ever been on the face of the Earth? I looked up and there, standing on the runway of an airport in Nigeria was a young man who had been a student teacher in my classroom the previous year. We greeted one another and in answer to my query, "What are you doing here?" he informed me that after graduation he had gone to work with an aid organization and had ended up here in northern Nigeria. The world continues to grow smaller.

Airport Bribery

When we left the airplane and entered the air terminal, we were immediately confronted by "customs officers", men in military uniforms who searched us and our luggage thoroughly. One of my strongest memories is the tribal scars apparent on the cheeks of these men. They had scars which made them look like they had feline whiskers; obviously intentionally carved in their faces when they were very young. They were not particularly friendly; however, we had no problems with them--yet.

A young man named Ali met us at the front entrance. He was to be our driver, provided by the University of Jos, for the next couple of months. He led us to his passenger van, a Toyota vehicle, helped us load our luggage and we were away. As the van reached the airport exit, we were stopped by armed guards. They too had the distinctive feline-like scars on their cheeks. They were demonstratively unfriendly. They demanded that all of us climb out of the bus in order that they could inspect our luggage and our passports. What was going on? As the leader of our group, I attempted to ask pertinent questions but was unceremoniously pushed aside. I finally went to Ali and asked him as quietly as I could what was happening. He smiled and told me that the guards, members of a tribe who had had reception rights for caravans crossing the Sahara Desert and arriving in Kano for hundreds of years, were looking for the traditional bribes which they deemed were their right. When I asked what type of bribes, he asked if we had any ballpoint pens. We had been advised to bring our own pens and consequently had a large box of Bics. I climbed back onto the bus, located the suitcase with our supplies, opened the box and grabbed a handful of the pens. I went then to the apparent leader of the guards and handed the pens to him. He literally beamed! Immediately we became the best of friends and were welcomed in Nigeria! With no further ado we were allowed to climb back on the bus and head down the highway to our future home away from home—Jos, Nigeria. So, that is how things were done in Nigeria.

The next couple of hours were reasonably uneventful; it was obvious that the government did not have a lot of money for highway maintenance and repair as the asphalt road was seriously eroded and full of potholes. The holes had been filled with crushed cans and other garbage and, as can be imagined, very rough. The sides of the road were littered with the burned out remains of vehicles which had been in accidents and left to lie derelict beside the highway. Twice on the approximately 250 kilometer trip to Jos, we were forced off the road by military vehicles approaching from the other direction. Military men on motorcycles waved us off the highway and we sat and watched pick-up trucks with large machine guns leading a motorcade of large, black Mercedes vehicles pass by. Ali explained that they were government officials who had the right of way on all highways.

Living in Nigeria

We were taken to a large house on the outskirts of Jos which would be our home for the next several weeks. We were impressed with the large, roomy building and the smaller guest houses which made up our compound. The house had been built in the 1950's for a British mining engineer who had administered many of the tin mines which were located in the area. When the British left Nigeria in 1960, the house was taken over by the university and was kept up and used to house visitors to the university. The house had a large living area, three bedrooms, kitchen and bathroom; a cook and three houseboys were also provided for our comfort. Two of us took up accommodation in the house and the other two professors, with their children, were accommodated in the guest houses on the property.

The University of Jos

Upon visiting the university the following day, we were surprised to see a reasonably large campus, composed of several long, single-storied, cinder brick, tin-roofed buildings. These were the classrooms, and, while not very plush, certainly were suitable for teaching. Well, perhaps that is a slight exaggeration; upon entering the classrooms, we discovered the desks were very old, tin chairs with small writing areas attached. Most were in serious disrepair and, as we were to find out later, had sharp edges that could at the least snag clothing and at the worst cut flesh. Each classroom had a blackboard at the front of the room, hanging on the wall—however, upon closer scrutiny, it was apparent they were simply sheets of half inch plywood which had been painted black. Water had seeped into most of them and the wood was swollen and rough. The black paint was flaked and peeling from the boards. The only chalk we were able to find was very soft; writing on the boards was an exercise in futility as the chalk quickly disappeared and the writing was nearly impossible to see.

The administrative offices appeared reasonably modern and, although we were visiting professors, were not available to us. Each of the desks had a telephone, but we were to find out that none of them worked. The wires had been buried under the ground when the buildings were built, and, in the years since the British had left, most of them had been compromised by seeping water. Because no one had a map of the underground system and, it was reported, the expertise to deal with it anyhow, the telephone system was only for show. Another showpiece was the large, top of the line, Xerox copying machine which stood in the main office. The machine was spotless and obviously, well-maintained. And then a secretary told us that it had never made a single copy. When it was delivered to the university a couple of years earlier, it had come without toner and they had not yet been able to have toner delivered to the university. Once again, an impressive piece of equipment but a useless office tool intended to make a good impression on visitors.

Fortunately for us we were taken care of by our cooks and houseboys. They lived in small houses on the estate which were located behind the large house. These quarters were mean; one or two rooms, often with dirt floors were the norm. Our head houseboy was married with four wives even though he was relatively young—in his middle twenties. He was very efficient and his wives served as the cooks. The meals they prepared were generally very good, that is, they were edible. While vegetables, fruit and rice were abundant, meat was a far scarcer commodity. Beef was generally served but once a week and was often so tough that one could not easily chew it. Well, one could chew it, but not swallow it. I found that it was good to chew long enough to get the flavor, but that the gristle and sinews would eventually have to be spit out. We occasionally had pork on our plates, but it was usually just small pieces which had been boiled in order to make them digestible. Chicken was served most often. But, believe it or not, the chicken too was so tough that one had to hope to get a piece from the breast, wing or back. The legs were like the beef and had to be chewed for the flavor and then spit out. Cattle in Nigeria were herded by nomads of the Fulani tribe (you have seen the pictures of cattle with large horns which grow straight up from the head and which are herded usually by teen-age boys, barefoot with a blanket for weather protection). We named these Fulani cattle, and eventually we named the chicken Fulani chicken too—they were equally difficult to chew.

Popcorn Snacks

The kitchen was not particularly sanitary. When we traveled to Nigeria, I packed popcorn kernels as a potential treat as I had been told that very little 'snack' food was available. After a full week in Nigeria, on the first Friday evening, after all of the house workers had left, we had a small party in our living room to celebrate the successful completion of the first week; I decided to pop some popcorn for a special treat. I got the kernels out of my luggage and went into the kitchen. As I turned on the light, the floor and counter tops seemed to move out of the way! I was shocked and quickly realized that I was looking at literally thousands of cockroaches! And most were not the small, insect-like cockroaches I was used to back in Canada, but were indeed two and three inches long. They were so-called flying cockroaches and were everywhere. They moved back into the walls and under the floor when the lights came on. Well, rather than exciting and upsetting my colleagues, I decided to proceed with my original plan—to make a popcorn treat for all. First thing, I had to find some cooking oil. I looked in the cupboards, the refrigerator and on the shelves. There seemed to be no oil of any type anywhere, but because I knew they had to have cooking oil somewhere, I continued my search. Finally, I noticed a couple of large, old cooking oil cans lying against the wall in the pantry; I lifted one and realized that it contained oil. I took it to the stove and poured oil into a pot I had found to pop the corn. As the oil poured out, it was black and as dirty as it could possibly be—not only that, large lumps, which I quickly discovered were dead cockroaches, fell into the pan. I nearly gave up my plan to provide a snack for my friends then and there, but in the end, decided that when the oil boiled, it would sterilize itself. And so, I was able to offer my colleagues a treat, popcorn which they all ate and appreciated. For the next several weeks, every Friday evening, I would go through the same process again, and, even though friends offered to help me prepare the popcorn, I turned them down. Finally, on the final Friday evening of our Nigerian experience, I asked them to all come into the kitchen to observe the preparation of the popcorn. When the lights came on and the cockroaches began to move, the screams and invectives were colorful. When I poured the oil into the pot, most of my colleagues left the room. Many of them would not share popcorn with me that evening and I experienced some severe criticism for providing them that 'treat' at all. Some people just can't be satisfied!

Western Shopping

In Nigeria it was difficult to buy groceries and supplies. There was only one so-called western shop in the city (a city of nearly one million people) where we could buy food stuffs that had been imported from the west. Needless to say, these canned goods were severely expensive and quite limited. Nevertheless, most Saturdays we would get Ali to drive us the forty minutes to the store and we would do some shopping. Entering the shop was difficult. Nigerians congregated in front of the store to beg where 'rich' westerners would shop. Unfortunately it was not only children doing the begging, but the crippled and maimed people of Jos of whom there were hundreds. Stepping over people who were blind (a common malady because of the tsetse flies), crippled (missing limbs, malformed limbs, birth defects) and disease ridden (leprosy, fevers, and various plagues) was not easy for us to do. We unfortunately probably encouraged the begging because we would usually empty our pockets of coins, gum and pens when we left the shop.

The only item which was always available was alcohol. Beer, wine and hard liquor were available in this shop and we kept ourselves reasonably well supplied. The beer was amazing. There were two brands readily available, Rock and Star. These beers, which came in large, one liter bottles, were amazingly good. I came to find out that the breweries had been in Nigeria since early in the twentieth century. They were originally built and administered by Scandinavians who were experts at their craft. Even though the administration of the breweries was taken over by Nigerians after 1960, they had learned the practice well and brewed excellent beer. Wines were imported, and generally were quite expensive. I remember spending the equivalent of $150.00 in Naira (the national currency) apiece for two bottles of Chateneauf de Pape, beautiful French wines. The whiskies, rum and vodka came with brand names I had never heard of but seemed nevertheless quite palatable. There was a locally brewed whiskey that was dirt cheap and which was quite difficult to drink, but we had to try everything at least once.

Teaching at University

My teaching assignment at the University of Jos was educational administration. I taught two courses (approximately 45 students in each class) for masters' degree candidates and one course (20 students) for doctoral students. The students were so keen and committed; I worked very hard to ensure that all of my lectures were well-prepared and meaningful. Working in the classroom conditions already described proved a challenge, but the results were gratifying. During the lectures, the students pulled the decrepit old tin desks as close as possible to the front of the classroom and tried to take down every word I spoke. They were such motivated students that I could only marvel at their dedication. Usually by the end of every lecture, I had only about three feet of space in which to speak and write on the horrible blackboard. When the class was finished, I gave the students my lecture notes which were then copied laboriously word-for-word and distributed to the members of the class. When I finally left the university to travel back to Canada, I distributed all of my clothing to members of the class as well. Such beautiful people!

More Bribery

At the time when we first arrived in Nigeria and after we finally made the connection between the officers and Bic pens, we held a meeting and discussed the concept of bribes, or as the Nigerians say, "Dash". We agreed that gift-giving is an accepted practice in social relationships around the world and that in various traditional societies it can take a number of forms. In Nigeria, its simplest form appeared to be a handout, usually solicited by a young person who accosted a person and invited a 'dash'. Our experiences in Jos when shopping at the western shop reflected clearly this type of transaction. However, the next level up was an invitation to give something (i.e. Bic pens) for which something was given in return (customs officers checking us into the country). This is likely a traditional practice in which there is a two-way obligation which some of us did not have the experience to recognize and we therefore insisted on conducting ourselves as if we were in Canada. We had difficulty recognizing that there was often a reciprocity involved that would often make the word 'bribe' inappropriate as an English translation. Unfortunately, we decided to take an inflexible, moral position irrespective of the situation which, in retrospect, was turning a blind eye to the local culture—daring to make value judgments on another culture in terms of our Canadian culture. We were probably correct in believing that there is a negative ethical dimension in providing "dash", but it is without doubt dependent on a correct understanding of the motivations of the recipients. At any rate, we decided as a group to forego the temptations of giving or receiving 'dash'. When we were ready to leave Nigeria, we realized we should have studied and attempted to better understand the concept of bribery.

All of us were excited about the prospect of completing our contracts and leaving Nigeria. The anticipation of the day of exit continued to build over the final weeks of our stay until, when the day arrived, we could hardly contain ourselves. We arose very early in the morning, said "Goodbye" to the good friends we had made during our stay, climbed on the van with our significantly lighter luggage (all of us having given away all but our essential clothing and toiletry items) and headed for the big city of Kano and the international airport there.

We had not had an opportunity to check on our departure tickets, but because it was long before etickets, we had paper tickets in hand. We arrived at the airport very early in the morning, and, although we were generally on different flights, some to Europe, some to Lagos and others to Kenya, our flights were scheduled for late afternoon. Inasmuch as we all had more than six hours to spend before departure, we were prepared to stand in line as long as was necessary to obtain our boarding passes. When we finally found the appropriate line up of people who were leaving Nigeria on international flights that day, we were somewhat disgruntled to realize that the line was several hundred people long and that it wound, snake-like, through the whole terminal. And, it was only one of many lines which intertwined throughout the terminal. However, we had time.

After standing in line for more than an hour and having hardly moved from the spot we started, we began to get nervous. It was obvious that the people who had paid 'dash' were being moved to the front of the line. We discussed the situation and decided that we should remain true to our principles and not pay anyone a bribe. As the morning grew older, more and more people moved ahead of us in line and we began to question the veracity of our group decision.

Our ultimate goal, the window where we would receive boarding passes, was an oblong-shaped hole cut into a sheet of very cheap wall board— on a severe bias. It did not instill confidence in us at all. After we had been waiting for two or three hours, we were suddenly surprised by the immediate stillness which settled over the waiting room. Through the front door of the terminal marched two uniformed, armed policemen. They headed in our direction and all of us began to fidget, wondering just what it was we had either done wrong or neglected to do. (Unfortunately, although I had not told my colleagues this, I was smuggling money out of Nigeria. I had taken ten one hundred US dollar bills into the country. Upon realizing that there was little to spend my money on, I determined to take eight bills back out of the country with me. However, once in Nigeria, I was told that it was illegal to take cash, in whatever currency, out of the country. In fact, the punishment was severe and involved incarceration in a Nigerian prison where no white man would ever expect to last more than a couple of weeks. Nevertheless, I determined to take my money with me and decided to smuggle it out. I used the back cardboard cover of a writing tablet; splitting the cardboard sheet in half using a razor blade, I secreted the bills inside and then glued the sheet back together. I then inserted the back of the tablet into a vinyl cover in which it fitted, and believed that it was impossible to see.) My guilty conscience went into overdrive and I was sure the policemen were coming for me. Much to my relief, the officers stopped in front of a young Nigerian woman in a line two rows over from us. They began to scream at her and were obviously demanding something—we were unsure what. She returned their screams with even louder screams of her own and the situation began to look grim. All of a sudden, one of the policemen hit the woman alongside her head with his nightstick—a gruesome cudgel made of hardened, black rubber. She went down as if she had been pole-axed and was dead to the world. The officers lifted her dress, found a wallet attached to her upper thigh and immediately grabbed it. They opened it, took out a number of Nigerian bills, threw the wallet back onto her body and left the building! Later, after she had somewhat recovered, we learned that she had promised to 'dash' the guards to enter the building and that she had neglected to do so. They took the money they felt was their due.

People continued most of the day to go to the head of the line; we began to think that even though we had tickets, there would be no more seats on the airplanes once we reached the window. Fortunately, after standing in line more than five hours, we reached the crooked window and spoke to the airline official working there. He was very kind and polite and told us we had nothing to worry about; because we had booked and paid for our tickets so far in advance, those seats would be held for us until the very last minute. Relief! He issued us boarding passes and waved us through a doorway into the departure area. I, being a smuggler, was nervous, especially when I recognized the workers with the cat's whiskers carved into their cheeks. However, they took my suitcase, placed it on a table and immediately marked it with a check in chalk. They then instructed me to put my briefcase, in which my money was hidden, on the table. The officer opened the briefcase, pawed through the contents, and then checked the outside with his trusty chalk. I was through!

I was directed to walk through an adjoining door, go up the stairs, walk through a connecting walkway and I would find myself in the departure lounge. I smiled, breathed a sigh of relief and headed up the stairs. As I moved down the walkway, two men in military uniforms, armed with rifles were walking towards me. As I moved to pass them, one of them told me to stand against the wall. The other held his rifle on me as the officer did a body search—through my clothes, thank goodness—looking for whatever. He touched every part of my body, including those areas we in the west consider intimate, and finally finished. It is obvious to me, on retrospect that the two were not necessarily looking for anything other than another bribe from me. They finally waved me on; I went down a flight of stairs, found myself in the departure lounge, immediately ordered two large Rock beers and drank them down without a breath. Whoa, what an experience! In a very short while I boarded the airplane and found myself on my way to Amsterdam and the real world.

Education, the type imparted while studying at university, does not prepare one for dealing with such incidents. It is possible that there should be education classes dealing with the propensity for students, teachers, parents, and yes, administrators to lie—or at least to embellish and distort the truth. It is true, that with experience, it becomes more possible to recognize untruths, half-truths and embellishments. However, an infallible method of making such determinations is sorrowfully absent. Unfortunately, the learning is in the experience—and often times the experience is too late for interventions of consequence.

CHAPTER IX

INTERNATIONAL EDUCATION – RUSSIA

Administration in Moscow

My first overseas experience as a principal occurred in Moscow, Russia, from 1994 through 1998. The school was pre-kindergarten through grade 8, located in a typical Russian school building built in the 1950's. We shared the school with a Japanese School which occupied the top two floors and a small Swedish School which was located in a small wing on the bottom floor. Our school, comprised of approximately 600 students, was located on the first three floors of the building. In addition, the pre-school, including a Reception class for four-year olds and three Kindergarten classes was located in a different building located about a ten minute walk across one of the busier thoroughfares in Moscow.

Replacing a Disgruntled Principal

Shortly after arriving in Moscow, my wife and I, after settling into our apartment with our two children, visited the school. Much to my chagrin, I discovered that the out-going principal, purportedly because of a dispute with the Director, had left the school with absolutely no pre-planning done. He had taken any class timetables, teacher lists, student lists and even supervision planning which had been created before the holidays, with him. Or, at least, these items were not to be found in the office. As can be imagined, with school scheduled to begin the following Monday, I went directly to work. I worked very hard for the next six days, designing an over-all school schedule, assigning teachers to classes, developing class lists of incoming and extant pupils, creating teacher supervision assignments, and actually planning a new school year from scratch—in a situation which was unfamiliar and even mysterious to me.

Summers in Moscow are warm and pleasant; we had no vehicle and so were forced to ride local busses to and from work during the first six weeks of our stay. Paperwork, including our permits to reside in the country had to be finalized before we would be allowed to purchase a car or make any other type of contractual commitment.

By the time the first day of school arrived, I felt that the school was at least ready to begin. That first day was a nightmare; many of the teachers arrived in Moscow just hours before the first day of classes, and as one could easily imagine, many of the returning teachers were dissatisfied with their teaching assignments, class lists and even classrooms. Unfortunately, many attributed the problems to the "new guy", instead of immediately recognizing that the former principal had sabotaged the school startup. Nevertheless, with patience, concentration and hard work, the "ruffled feathers" were smoothed, the scheduling conflicts were sorted out and the perceived affronts to teachers were remedied. Compounding the difficulties encountered that first day was the fact that our neighbor, the principal of the high school, had invited us to dinner the previous afternoon. He was a collector of vodka, and convinced me, albeit with significant trepidation, to taste several of his twenty-seven varieties of Russian "water of life". Another valuable lesson learned…

School Security in Moscow

Moscow in the mid-nineties was an emerging free-market. The city was not particularly safe, and together with the so-called "Russian Mafia" and corrupt politicians, life often verged on the dangerous. Occasional car bombings, assassination attempts on bankers and kidnappings were constantly in the news. Consequently, even though our school and its grounds were surrounded by a ten foot high fence, nevertheless, it was necessary to remain vigilant and to be aware of what was transpiring around us in the city of Moscow. As a new principal, the safety of students and faculty was of major concern to me. In order to instill a sense of security in our school environment, I made it a practice from the first day onward to meet all of the students at the front gate of the school as they entered the school grounds. The only bus transportation to the school came from the United States Embassy and accounted for approximately one third of our student population. All of the other students, between 300 and 500 students, arrived by automobile. Many of the cars were driven by mothers, but the vast majority was driven by hired Russian drivers. The traffic on the small one-lane road in front of the school was horrendous—morning and afternoon. As the school principal, although I represented the authority for the school, nevertheless, without the advantage of speaking Russian, I often encountered difficult and potentially unsafe situations with the drivers. Keeping the traffic flow moving and, at the same time, ensuring that students were able to get out of vehicles and enter the school grounds safely required concentration and dedication. It was another new role in the litany of requirements for the principal.

One of the most difficult situations arose often when a particularly large vehicle, driven by a burly, flat-topped Russian would arrive. The young girl, who was being driven to school by this fellow, was the daughter of an influential banker in the city of Moscow. In addition to the driver, one other ominous-looking fellow always climbed out of the vehicle and accompanied her to the school gates. It was obvious that these two men were not only her driver, but her body-guards. They wore large bulky overcoats which often would gap open to provide me with a look at their pistols in shoulder-holsters. For the first few days, they would attempt to walk into the school grounds with the young girls; I immediately stopped them and politely explained that they were not allowed on the property while carrying weapons. They were unhappy about this and shortly thereafter I received a telephone call from the girl's father. I explained to him the situation and from that day on, the men would stop at the front gate and continue to watch the girl until she either entered the school or disappeared around the corner of the building as she went to the playground. In the meantime, all of the traffic on the small road would be backed up until they moved their vehicle.

Traffic control in front of the school was another new responsibility for the principal. The small, narrow road required a firm hand and strong voice. Without this type of supervision, chaos and long waits were the result. I certainly had learned nothing about this in university.

Security Stress

An interesting incident occurred when one of our teachers visited this family in their home. This family lived in a dacha community just outside of the Moscow city limits—very exclusive and heavily guarded. The teacher and her husband—he being an important business man—also lived in a dacha in the area. They one day were walking their dog—a large Irish setter—when they inadvertently passed the home of the banker. The parents saw them walking down the roadway and sent one of their men to invite them into the home for tea. They accepted the invitation and, accompanied by several men, entered the home. Their dog was left outside to fend for itself and they sat down with the husband and wife to have a cup of tea. Several of the men stood around in the room as they waited for the tea to steep, and the circumstances seemed somewhat awkward. All of a sudden, their dog, concerned about their absence, ran around the dacha and, spying a large window, stood on its hind legs to peer into the house. Of course, being a large dog and having big feet with long toe nails, when the dog's feet hit the window, it made a large rattling sound which resounded through the room where tea was being served. The teacher told me that they were left sitting alone on their chairs in the room--everyone else, including all of the men and the father and mother, had hit the floor and pulled guns which they had aimed at the dog. The incident occurred so quickly that they didn't have time to react, but somehow everyone else in the room hit the deck! So much for safety and security in the Russian capital.

Expatriate Parents

Dealing with the normal incidents and situations which occur in schools was complicated in an international school by the insistent involvement of parents in their children's education. Because most of the students' fathers were in Russia because they were involved in their work—business, media, embassies, consulates, etc.—mothers were often left at home with little to occupy their time. Consequently, because school is something they understand and have an affinity with, most wanted to be involved in the operation of the school. (I have the opinion that many families who lived internationally in places like Moscow, had conscience twinges regarding their children. Too many believed that they were providing their children with experiences that were not consistent with those they would have had in their home countries and therefore were somewhat overprotective of them. It takes strong educators, teachers and administrators alike, to deal with the sometimes aggressive nature of parents in this situation.)

Now don't get me wrong—it was great to have so many parents involved in the school--in particular those who were realistic and actually helpful. Parental involvement was something we had always strived to promote in the schools back in Canada, and it was not always easy to achieve. Ongoing parental involvement comes with its own disadvantages—constant complaining, teachers under constant pressure, students wishing their parents were not so involved, parents believing they know better about how students learn—well, you get the idea. Most parents, after involving themselves with teachers in the classroom, must speak with the principal. A considerable amount of my administrative time was devoted to parent meetings. Eventually, after I finally figured out what it was parents were asking for, I was able to deal with their issues through exerting patience (listening to their concerns), empathizing with their family situations, and finally convincing them that they had the very same educational goals for their children that we in the school were promoting and that we should work together to achieve those goals. Once parents realized they had an empathetic and sympathetic ear in the school, they were much happier and supportive.

Family Issues

Having your own family in the school where you are principal brings its own problems. I have been fortunate that my wife, a talented, capable and experienced teacher, understood the difference in roles we played in the school. She was willing to allow me to function as the "boss" without interfering in my responsibilities. I likewise was able to leave her to her own devices—which was being the best teacher she could be without interference from me. However, many times she had to endure the frustrations of entering a room of teachers only to have the conversations stop—a good indicator that the school's administration was the topic. However, once they realized that she was not a "plant", they were able to accept her as a colleague. The life of the principal's wife is not always easy.

My Son, the Fighter

It is obvious that the principal's children were also plagued because of their relationship to the head of the school. My children have told me that many times their friends made their lives difficult by making reference to their parents—usually when an issue was being dealt with. On one memorable occasion, I learned one of the more important lessons about having one's own children in the school. When I arrived in the Moscow school, after encountering some difficulties with bullying and fighting among the children—often caused by the more than forty different nationalities and cultures—I made the decision to eliminate all violence from the school. In order to enforce this edict, I informed everyone that fighting and bullying would result in immediate suspension from school for all parties involved. Students would only be allowed back into school and their classes after serving the suspension (usually three days) and after a meeting had been held with the student and their parents.

Of course, as fate would have it, the day arrived when a bully had an altercation with my son. I have forgotten the detail of the situation, however, my son was in the fourth grade and a new boy in his class had proven himself over several weeks to be a bully by picking on several members of the class. One day my son and others, this boy included, were playing corner ball—a game where they were bouncing a ball back and forth to one another. The new boy was making his presence known by pushing others around, swearing at them and trying to dominate the game. Eventually he pushed my son and threatened him. My son, while not normally aggressive, endured the hassling and verbal abuse for as long as he could take it. And then, he doubled up his fist and hit the boy in the nose. Apparently, it was at this juncture that the teacher on playground duty noticed the altercation and interceded. I was in my office working on something. All of a sudden the door opened and the teacher hauled two crying and struggling boys into my office. One of them had a bloody nose and the other—was my son!

As was my wont, I settled the boys into two different chairs, heard the report from the teacher, and then listened to the two sides of the story. Without going into detail, the boys described the circumstance as they remembered it—with significant embellishments, I'm sure—and then waited for the response. They were both suspended for three days!

This was not a major incident in and of itself in the accumulated years of my principal experiences. However, it was a major incident in my son's school life and in my role as father. My son and I discussed the situation on several occasions, usually ending in tears and realizing that we had both experienced a situation which would impact our lives for years to come. In fact, recently in a telephone conversation, my son referred to this incident as an important experience in his life. He is now twenty-two years of age. Because I didn't waiver in my administration of punishments just because my own flesh and blood was involved, this incident did have a serious impact on the culture of the school. Students, teachers and even parents realized that rules were made for everyone and the imposing of punishments could not be influenced by extraneous circumstances—not even blood relationships.

Diverse Culture Issues

The diverse cultures in an international school create situations for administrators as well. It was not unusual for the parents of Asian students, upon coming into the school for the first time, to bring presents for the principal! This of course was an experience alien to my thinking and many times I felt myself in an awkward position when I turned down a gift. I remember parents offering me a beautiful wristwatch on one occasion which was obviously far more valuable than any I had ever owned before. I was tempted to accept the gift for just a second, but as politely as I could, turned it down, indicating that it was against my personal and professional policy to accept gifts. The parents left my office somewhat disgruntled, and I wasn't sure whether I had insulted them or not. These were difficult situations. It was not much later in that school year when I was informed by a classroom teacher that a young boy in her class was being physically abused at home. When I brought this ten year old boy into my office and interviewed him, he told me that his father would beat him if he got poor grades—poor being a relative term, but anything less than perfect would qualify—and that he therefore had bruises. When his father and mother came into my office, I realized that they were the same parents who had tried to present me with a gold watch. I was pleased to know that I had not accepted that gift as I had a very difficult time convincing these parents that physical abuse was not acceptable treatment of students in western schools. I had to maintain my position with them and had I accepted a valuable gift from them earlier in the year, this would have been doubly difficult.

My Daughter Meets the Queen

In October of our first year in Moscow, Queen Elizabeth of England came to visit with Boris Yeltsin in Moscow. This visit was newsworthy because she was the first reigning British monarch to ever visit Russia. Of course, because of the upcoming visit, there was a great deal of excitement and preparation in the British community. As nearly a third of our students were British, a flurry of activities took place, including a planned field trip for all British students to observe the queen as she was visiting St. Andrews Cathedral in Moscow.

On Wednesday morning, the 19th of October, our school vans were reserved to take all of the British students into the center of Moscow. The meeting place was in front of the main school. As was our normal morning routine, I and my family arrived at the school early. Our daughter, who at the time was four years old and attending the Reception class in the other building, arrived and began to play with her good friend, the son of a BBC journalist. Typically they would play together for about a half hour, then would board the school van and be transported to the other building. Of course, on this particular morning, the vans were designated to take the British students downtown. As one of the British teachers accompanying the students saw our daughter and her friend playing, she assumed they were both British and that they too should get on the bus. Now all of the British children had dressed in their best 'bib and tucker' to visit the queen, but our daughter had dressed herself that morning—she was quite independent and strong-willed. Her costume was quite outlandish and certainly not representative of her nicest clothes. At any rate, when the teacher insisted they climb on the bus, she accompanied her friend as was her normal routine. The bus left the school and headed downtown.

In the meantime, while involved in a variety of other duties, I realized that it was time for me to drive my daughter to the other school because the school vans were otherwise occupied. When I looked around the playground, she was nowhere to be seen. We were relatively new to Moscow and very concerned about the safety and well-being of our children; I began to panic. After asking everyone in the area whether they had seen our daughter, they indicated that they had not. Finally, one teacher suggested that she thought she may have seen her boarding one of the vans with her friend. I immediately made the decision to ask one of the school drivers to drive me into the city in order to verify that she had gone on the fieldtrip—and that she had not indeed not wandered off or, worse yet, been kidnapped. We took off and within fifteen minutes were caught up in one of the major traffic jams that only can happen in Moscow.

As I sat in the car and fretted for the next ninety minutes or so, the bus carrying my daughter and her friends arrived in the area of St. Andrews Cathedral; the students were allowed to disembark from the bus and to line the street where the queen would walk after visiting the cathedral. So, here they were, the British students in their very best finery and our daughter, in a haberdasher's nightmare of contrasting garish colors and patterns, lined up on the side of the road to see the queen. One of the teachers, recognizing that our daughter was small, moved her to the very front of the rows of people lining the streets. When the queen and the archbishop of the church came out onto the street, the people cheered and clapped. The queen moved slowly down the rows of people, and when she arrived at the point where my daughter was standing, she stopped, looked down, smiled and patted her on the head! However, our daughter, more interested in the fellow with the funny hat, put her hand up and tried to move the old lady in the fancy hat out of her way so she could see the archbishop. And I know all of this to be true, because, eventually, the father of her friend sent me a videotape of the incident which had been filmed for the BBC! A snapshot of the moment also surfaced and became a part of that year's yearbook.

A couple of hours later we were happily reunited at the school; our daughter was quite taken aback at our tearful reunion and couldn't understand the amount of excitement her spontaneous fieldtrip had caused. Because we were so concerned, it obviously scared her and she would not talk about nor acknowledge her fieldtrip for several years. I must admit that for about three hours that morning I was more a father than a principal!

CHAPTER X

INTERNATIONAL EDUCATION – SAUDI ARABIA

Administration in Saudi Arabia

After four years in Moscow, my wife and I accepted positions in Saudi Arabia with another international school. We sought new positions at a job fair on the east coast of the United States, and, even though we were offered more than one position, we opted for Saudi Arabia because we believed the schools there offered better opportunities for our children.

The contrasts between Russia and Saudi Arabia were significant. Moving from a northern climate to a desert was the first major change. When we arrived in Jeddah, as we stepped from the airplane, the heat radiating off the runway early in August nearly melted us. The temperature was near 40 degrees Celsius and the sun was blinding. We definitely had a lot to learn about living in one of the hotter climates in the world.

We had accepted positions in a smaller Saudi city about a hundred miles north of the ancient city of Jeddah. This city was nearly a thousand miles distant from the school central offices which were located on the eastern coast of the Kingdom. This then, was the second major contrast—no longer did we have the support of the central offices and personnel of the school in the same city, but in fact we were isolated on the west coast—the nearest support being several hours away.

The housing was a change as well; no longer did we live in an apartment in a high rise as in Moscow, but now we moved into the world of compound living. Our three-bedroom unit, with western appliances, two floors and two bathrooms, was situated behind a high wall in a compound built to accommodate westerners living in the Kingdom. Our swimming pool was located immediately in front of our home and our western neighbors were close by.

The school was perhaps the best school facility I had ever worked in; it had more than thirty large classrooms, well-equipped teachers' lounge, an auditorium, an outdoor swimming pool, enormous art and music rooms, a sports gymnasium large enough to accommodate hundreds of spectators for sporting events; a separate building for the early-childhood classes, roofed outdoor playing areas for the students and the most abundant supply of learning and teaching materials I had ever encountered.

Shipment and Saudi Bureaucracy

As my family and I first arrived in the Kingdom, we were coming from Moscow, Russia where we had spent the previous four years. Naturally, the accumulations of personal items which we had gathered during those four years were significant. The school in Moscow had a generous shipping allowance and we sent these items ahead to Saudi Arabia. Obviously there were many items which could not be sent into Saudi and we were diligent in assuring that such items (alcohol, Christmas decorations, Christian religious items, etc.) were not included in the shipment. As soon as we arrived in the Kingdom, we received notice that our shipment had arrived in the port of Jeddah and that we would soon be able to take delivery of the same. The shipment contained our computer, books, pots and pans, clothing, knick-knacks, CDs, and various other items. We were already eagerly anticipating the delivery of our possessions as we knew that they would help us adjust to living in a new culture that much more quickly. Imagine our surprise when a couple of days later we received news through the government relations office of our school district that alcohol had been discovered in our shipment and it would not be delivered to us! I immediately contacted the head of the office and assured him in no uncertain terms that there was no alcohol in our shipment. He agreed to pursue the matter. Over the next several weeks, we received little information regarding the status of our shipment and began to feel very uneasy. After many telephone calls and emails near the end of September, the assistant superintendent in charge of the government relations office paid me a visit. Inasmuch as our school was about a thousand miles away from district office, the visit was a surprise. The assistant superintendent came to my office and told me that I would have to sign a document indicating that I had indeed attempted to ship alcohol into the Kingdom in order for the shipment to be released. He further informed me that the government would pardon me for breaking the law this time, but that the incident would always be associated with my name in future dealings with the government. I was incensed! I knew I had done no such thing and I informed him that under no circumstance would I sign such an admission. He advised me to sign the document, or I would have to accept that my shipment could be confiscated and I might be forced to pay a fine in order to be allowed to remain in the Kingdom! I refused. The assistant superintendent (who was a Saudi citizen) and I had a difficult conversation as he obviously believed that the accusation was true—for whatever reason.

After he had left and traveled back to the other side of the Kingdom, I had telephone conversations with my new boss, the superintendent, and I informed him that I was prepared to have my contract nullified rather than sign a document admitting to a transgression that I had not committed. Finally, after several days, I spoke with the assistant superintendent again and insisted that I was going to travel to Jeddah to see the alleged alcohol for myself and that I wanted him to make the necessary arrangements with the customs' officials. I booked a flight during the second week of October and prepared to fly south. About two hours before my flight was to depart, I received a call from the assistant superintendent. He said, "I have wonderful news. The customs officials are now saying that the alcohol was in the shipment next to yours—your shipment will be released shortly." Well, I was still not sure what to think of this development. However, I am inclined to believe that this was the end of an elaborate attempt to extort money out of me in order to have my shipment released. Who were involved in the extortion attempt? I can't say as I was kept physically away from the officials in charge—but I have my suspicions.

As denouement to this incident, our shipment was delivered to our compound the following week. All of the items in the shipment had been trashed. The hard drive of my computer was destroyed. Our used clothing was ripped and dirty. Many of our CDs were missing or scratched horribly. Some glass angels that my wife had shipped from Moscow had had their wings broken off and taped to the bodies! In the end, the majority of our items had to be thrown away. I received a bill which I had to pay for importing used clothing, pots and pans, and home decorations into the Kingdom! None of the other westerners in our community had had to pay money to receive their items. Another lesson learned!

Political Contacts

Not too long after our arrival in Saudi, one of our assistant superintendents, a Saudi national, wanted to take me to visit the mayor of our city. It apparently was not necessary to make an appointment; it was normal to show up and be invited into the mayor's office. As we moved through various offices, in most cases with armed Saudi policemen in evidence, I realized that my colleague had come prepared. He dispersed gifts wherever we went, in most cases, bottles of perfume and aftershave lotion. The various officials seemed genuinely pleased to welcome us into their offices, and finally, we found ourselves in the office right outside the office of the mayor. We sat for several minutes, waiting apparently for the moment when it would be proper to enter the mayor's presence. Eventually we were ushered into a large, sumptuous office. The walls had tapestry-like hangings, but, naturally, without any depiction of living things. A large trophy cabinet was located against one wall and it contained numerous plaques and trophies. Red velvet chairs were situated around the walls and at the far end, behind a large mahogany desk, sat the mayor. Many of the chairs around the room were occupied by Saudi men, all dressed in the typical fashion, thobe, red-checkered gutra and igal (the black rope holding the gutra onto the top of the head). Most of the men were elderly, that is, they had white beards, some of which were henna red. Those with red beards did not have an igal on their gutras, and their red-checkered head scarves were carefully ironed and hung from their heads down their chests. The thobes these men were wearing were noticeably shorter, reaching only the tops of their ankles—contrasting with the normal length of the thobes of most Saudi men. We went to all of these men, and shook their hands. Each of them uttered, "Salaam al Leikam" to which I responded (after significant coaching from my colleague), "Al Leikam Salaam". We then turned to the mayor who remained standing behind his very large desk. We shook hands with him and were then seated in two chairs immediately in front of his desk. The mayor was a relatively younger man—I would estimate about forty years old. He had a black beard and was dressed like all of the others, except his gutra was white, not red checkered. I learned later that he, a member of the Royal Family, was one of the many princes in the Kingdom. The position as mayor of the city was an appointment because of his heritage. As we took our seats, the man from the front office entered with cardamom coffee and dates which he placed on the desk in front of us.

Over the next several minutes, the mayor asked me several questions about the school—what was the population; how many foreign teachers; how much was the tuition, and so on. My colleague from the superintendent's office acted as interpreter. It seemed obvious that the mayor was not conversant in English and I, of course, was severely limited in my Arabic. The visit seemed to go quite well, and I received the impression that the mayor truly welcomed the presence of the 'western' school in the city and that he understood it played a significant role in the lives of the many western employees of the large oil companies which dominated the economy of the city.

Mid-way through this discussion, another elderly man entered the office. He came immediately towards us, first greeting the mayor with kisses to the cheeks and on the nose, and then shook our hands. He too was dressed in the shorter thobe and his checkered gutra sported no igal. After shaking my hand, he said to me in impeccable English, "Very nice to meet you, Mr. Bowen. We welcome you to the Kingdom. Should you have any issues, please do not hesitate to contact my office." I was very surprised and stammered, "Thank you. It is a pleasure to be here." He then said something very strange, "Yes, we have been aware of you since the day you arrived and we perceive that you are comfortable here." He then turned and, after greeting the other men in the room, took a seat.

The mayor took the opportunity through my interpreter to admonish me to encourage everyone in our school and the community to adhere to the laws of Islam and to not create any issues within the city. We were obviously dismissed, and as we turned to go, after once again shaking hands with the men in the office, the mayor said, "Do you like the Pittsburg Steelers?" I nearly fell to the floor. His English was very North American and totally colloquial. When I expressed my surprise, he laughed and said, "I studied at the University of Pennsylvania for my doctorate and became a real fan of professional football."

When we reached our car outside, I could contain myself no longer and asked my colleague who the old man was who had spoken to me in such good English, and what had he meant by saying that he was aware of my presence. My colleague laughed and told me that I had just met the head of the secret police for the western part of Saudi Arabia. Hm. I asked about the dress differences, short thobe, no igal, etc. and was told that these men were part of the infamous Saudi Matawa, the so-called religious police. They wore clothes that were slightly different than the normal costume as they believed more firmly that the Koran dictated exactly what and how they should wear their clothes. Apparently there is no mention of the igal in the Koran and thobes are described as being shorter than what is normally seen.

Religious Police

We had heard many stories of the Matawa, generally negatively disposed toward westerners. They are the persons who police the people in adherence to Islamic principles: attending prayer, women not walking by a mosque with their hair uncovered or with any of their body showing; women not associating with males not of their family; etc. They generally carry a supple wooden wand with which they will tap offending persons. My wife and I, on our first trip to Jeddah, had gone to a mall to buy some needed school supplies. We were in a book store, my wife wearing modest western clothes, when the clerk, a young man from Sri Lanka, all of a sudden told my wife to get into the back room behind a curtain. Shortly thereafter, an ancient Matawa policeman stuck his head in the shop and yelled at the clerk, telling him it was time to close the store for afternoon prayers. After he left, the young man told us that this particular Matawa was very mean, especially to non-Muslims, and to avoid hassles, he had sent my wife, an obvious western woman, out of his sight.

Burglary

One morning when I arrived at the school, as I walked through the school greeting teachers and inspecting the premises, a teacher met me in the hallway outside of her classroom and told me that her printer was missing. I went into the room and immediately noticed that in addition to the missing printer, there was a mess of papers on the floor. It became immediately obvious, once we went around to the back of the school and found footprints in the sand leading to the back wall, that we had had a burglary—someone had crawled over our ten foot high wall, jimmied the back door to that wing of the school and had taken a color printer. Now, in the Kingdom, this type of thievery was not supposed to happen, but I, thinking I was doing the correct thing based on my recent meeting with the mayor, called the police. Within an hour, two uniformed policemen arrived at my office. I accompanied them to the classroom and they inspected the area and, upon realizing that we were telling the truth, indicated that they should call their supervisor. (I think a crime in the 'western' school was more than their training had prepared them for.) It was not long thereafter that a contingent of policemen arrived, all of them having to descend on the classroom where the crime had occurred. After much standing around and nodding and Arabic conversations, they decided they needed to make more telephone calls.

Around noon, the detective unit arrived at the school and went to the classroom with the fingerprinting equipment. I began to realize that the amount of 'angst' caused by reporting this crime was going to be more than the issue was worth. These fingerprint experts proceeded to cover the entire classroom with black powder. It should have been obvious to them that the room would be full of fingerprints—it was after all a classroom. Nevertheless, they spent the next couple of hours gathering their evidence. Finally, that afternoon, the chief of police entered my office. In Saudi, the officer's rank is indicated by the brass insignia on his shoulders. The chief had large crowns with knives rampant and there was no mistaking his authority. He immediately informed me that I should gather all of the janitorial staff into one room in order that they be questioned. Of course, the janitorial staff was composed of foreign workers—men from Bangladesh, Sri Lanka, India and the Philippeans. It had never occurred to me that Saudi nationals could not have possibly stolen anything. Even though I was able to point out the culprit's footprints at the back of the school, the chief was convinced that it was an 'inside job'.

When I told the head caretaker, Jack, to gather up the day crew and report to the library, he audibly gasped and said, "Mr. Bowen, I have to go home and tell the others that the police are coming." I responded, "No, the police only want to talk to you in the library." With fear in his voice and eyes, Jack said, "While they are talking to us here, they will go to our homes and search through our things. They have done this before and if they find alcohol, counterfeit videos, pictures of women or even religious paraphernalia, they will send us to jail." I said, "Go! And hurry back so they don't know you have gone!" Jack ran out the door and left in the white pickup. He told me later that even though he drove home as fast as he could, the police arrived at the same time he did. He ran into the house and warned the other men who were on afternoon shift. The police entered his apartment, immediately slapped his face, and pushed him around. They searched the various apartments looking for the printer, and when they didn't find it, they screamed at the workers and slapped them and pushed them. Eventually they put them in a vehicle and took them to the police station.

Several hours later that evening, Jack called me and told me what had happened. His workers were finally released and allowed to go to work. They were all accused of being the thief, but because there was no evidence, the police had to let them go.

Meanwhile, that afternoon, the chief of police held a meeting with the other workers in the school library. The meeting can best be described as an hour long demonstration of the power and authority of the police—physical abuse, verbal abuse and no opportunity for anyone to speak in the workers' defense. I finally realized that reporting a minor crime to the police was the wrong process to follow. Contrary to what I had been told in the mayor's office, the police were not really there to help us. Their methods were brutal and self-serving. I would know better the next time to not call on them for their support.

The chief of police came into my office after the library meeting and asked to speak with me. He then proceeded to inform me that the burglary was definitely undertaken by one of our foreign workers and that it would be well to have them all fired and deported back to their home countries. I was astounded by his declaration and suggested that we would continue looking into the situation. He told me that I would never get the truth out of persons such as these, and it would be far better to change my complete caretaking staff. He then told me that he just happened to have a company that would like to get the contract for cleaning my school! He was trying to turn the situation into a business deal for himself. Needless to say, I did not replace my cleaners, most of who had been working in the school for more than five years, and eventually the incident died down. However, the chief of police did visit me on several further occasions, each time attempting to get me to hire his company.

Wall Extension

Another consequence of the theft of a printer from our school resulted in significant time expenditure and cost. I was called to the Royal Commission (the civic governing body) for a meeting in which I was informed that, although the school property had a two meter wall completely surrounding it, nevertheless, I would be responsible for increasing the height of the wall by one meter. Several months of information gathering, planning meetings with staff, and meetings with Royal Commission engineers resulted in a costly construction project—the addition of a meter high extension on the top of the wall. Even though the extension was a requirement of the local government, nevertheless, the complete cost was to be borne by the school. Unfortunately, because our only income was tuition, and because such a significant expenditure had not been anticipated, the costs would impinge on the monies intended for education. It required significant financial planning and difficult cut-backs, not to mention a tuition increase (which is never well-received by parents and companies). For the next two years, the theft of a simple printer impacted negatively the education of more than five hundred students.

The city in which we lived was a custom-built city, built by the government of Saudi Arabia to provide a port on the Red Sea for shipping oil products. Although the old town had been there as far back in recorded history as records go (Ancient Egyptians had invaded the Saudi peninsula here in ancient times; Lawrence of Arabia had spent considerable time in the old town.), the new city had only existed for about twenty-five years. The government was put in place by the federal government and was called the Royal Commission. This government was responsible for the design, administration and policing of the city. Obviously, working closely with this governing body was important for the international school. To this end, the principal spent considerable time visiting and working with the heads of education in the Royal Commission. These men were powerful and important men in the Saudi community. They were the ones who decided where the international school would be located (our building was a Saudi school for which we paid a significant annual rent), what activities could be carried out there, what students could attend our school and what elements were necessary in our curriculum besides our western requirements (i.e. Arabic language, Islamic religion classes, etc.)

Public Meeting Embarrassment

In order to establish a closer working relationship with these important individuals, I came up with the idea to host an open-house for the heads of education and local government authorities. We planned a tour of our facilities including visits into classrooms while classes were in session, a luncheon and a presentation which would include short speeches by our district superintendent and me. In addition to the Saudi government officials, we invited high-ranking officials of western business operations, thinking it would be a good opportunity for these persons to meet one another outside of their official duties. When the day of the meeting arrived, we were prepared and looked forward to the visitations with significant anticipation.

The government official in charge of foreign education, that is, the western international school, was the assistant director of the entire Royal Commission. He was a congenial, highly educated and dedicated civil servant who earned more than a million dollars annually. I had had the pleasure of meeting with him many times in his office and had established what I believed was a close professional and personal relationship. He had attended university in the United States and was totally fluent in English. In addition to his position with the government, he also owned several businesses in the city. He was under pressure at this time to oversee and construct a series of statues in the new city, prior to an impending visit by the Crown Prince of Saudi Arabia

Islam does not allow the reproduction of living creatures in any form, consequently, most statues and monuments take the form of inanimate object, incorporating such items as cars, oil pipes, motors, bicycles, boats, palm trees, well, you get the idea. Naturally, even though many of these structures, at least to the western eye, are oddly put together, nevertheless, they have a significant role in the beautification of the cities. Jeddah, an ancient city on the west coast, has many examples of this phenomenon. Even though by western standards they may seem somewhat primitive, Arabic artists are hired at great expense to design and build them. A Royal visit to the city was fast approaching and several statues and monuments were to be designed and built prior to the Crown Prince's visit. Therein lay the pressure on this man.

As the meeting began, it was obvious that it had potential for success. Most of the invited Saudi officials arrived, partook of the coffee, tea and doughnuts and then accompanied us on a tour of the school and a first-hand look at western education in action. For most of the Saudis, this was the first opportunity they had had, even though the school had existed for more than ten years, to observe western education. The co-educational nature of our programs was for most of them an unusual and impressive educational experience. Saudi schools were of course, after the very early grades, segregated by gender.

Finally, we gathered in a large room and began the more formal part of the meeting. The superintendent spoke, talking about international education in the Kingdom generally, and then I, as the principal, made a presentation on our local programs and goals. When we had finished, we opened the meeting to questions. Many of the questions from the Saudi participants focused on the impact of western education, in particular technology, on the programs offered in the Saudi school systems and the implications for the future of education in the Kingdom. And then, the unthinkable… One of the western invitees, an engineer working for an oil company subsidiary, raised his hand to ask a question. He stood, and then in a seemingly condescending tone, said, "Well, if the Royal Commission and Saudi government would quit spending so much money on these ridiculous and childish statues, they would have money to invest in technology for the future of their children." This statement was wrong on many counts. Implying that the Saudi government was in any way wasting money; suggesting that the education of children was being neglected; implying that the planning and construction of statues and monuments were financially wasteful; and maintaining that the planning was less then professional and well planned were the obvious errors in judgment which this man demonstrated. There was a long pregnant pause as the negativity of his words sunk into the minds of those present, and then, the Assistant Director General of the Royal Commission stood up in the front row. He turned, faced the audience, and demanded, "I want the name of the man who just spoke and his iqama (Saudi work permit) number. And I want it immediately!" He then nodded at his colleagues and headed for the exit. Immediately two of the secret police approached the engineer and hustled him out of the room. I ran to intercept the Assistant Director General to try and persuade him that the man spoke inappropriately, and because it occurred in our meeting, to apologize for his words. He turned to me and said, "Mr. Bowen. We will meet in my office next week to discuss this incident." And with that, he and his entourage were gone.

Fortunately, when we met the following week, the Assistant Director General had calmed down, and even though he saw the incident as a direct insult to him, he claimed that he would not blame me or the western school for the affront. The engineer was sent, 'exit only', out of the country, and, for the next several months, relations with the Royal Commission were cool and occasionally frustrating.

Hand-Holding Onstage

Living in the Kingdom obviously meant significant changes to the lifestyle of western women. They were no longer able to drive a car, go out in public without being modestly covered, or even to teach in the same style they were used to. It was no different for my wife; she began her career in the Kingdom teaching music and quickly learned an interesting lesson.

The co-educational nature of our international school was very difficult for the Saudi authorities (and general population, I'm sure) to accept. The government went to great expense to build separate schools for boys and girls, and I have no doubts that our western practice of teaching boys and girls together was difficult for them to accept.

One incident stands out in my mind that brought the situation home to me. My wife, teaching music, and as was her wont, prepared a musical for parents which would be presented on stage in the month of February. February was a very busy time for me while working in international schools as it was the time of year when I attended international job fairs to hire teachers for the upcoming school year. I was in England recruiting teachers when my wife's musical hit the stage. It was a musical presentation put on by the younger students, Kindergarten through Grade four (5-9 year olds). Although I wasn't there to see it, I was told that it was cute and entertaining. During the final number, the boys and girls held hands and sang a song. Someone in the audience, a parent likely, didn't like that.

When I arrived back in the Kingdom early the next week, I had a note that I was to contact the police department in the Royal Commission. I called the number I had been given and when I reached the policeman, he informed me that I would have to report to the station immediately. Completely unaware of what kind of issue faced me, I drove immediately to the station and entered. I was immediately escorted to a small room and instructed to sit down on the chair in the middle of the room. I did so; the policeman escorting me left the room and locked the door. There were no windows and the door was locked. I therefore had to sit and wait patiently for something to happen. More than an hour later, the door opened and in walked a uniformed policeman, a Matawa (I could tell by his dress) and another man dressed in regular thobe and gutra. The man introduced himself as a detective and asked me to explain why I had acted against the laws of the Kingdom. I was totally taken unawares, and had no idea what he was referring to. Eventually, he told me that a concerned citizen had reported that I condoned the physical contact of boys and girls in my school. Even at this point I was confused as to what he was referring to, because I had not seen the musical presentation where the purported transgressions had occurred. Finally, he explained to me that boys and girls could not hold hands in a public place in the Kingdom and that they had done so during a musical presentation in my school. I as the principal was the person responsible, and to compound matters and make them worse, I was the husband of the woman who had caused the problem and responsible for her actions! I was to be arrested. I was totally confused, and, I must say, somewhat upset. We had all heard stories about how bad the conditions were in the Saudi jails and I certainly did not wish to spend time there. Although I tried to explain to them that the western school had dispensation to allow girls and boys to play and study together, they were not buying the explanation. I asked the police in desperation if they would please contact the Assistant Director General of the Royal Commission and explain what was happening. A short time later, the policemen reentered the room and released me. No explanations, apologies or admonitions were given—I was told to leave. I can only assume that my contact in the Royal Commission told them to release me.

Christmas Concert—An International Incident

About five years earlier, an incident had occurred which had not endeared the police to the western school. In December, the school was having an evening concert for the parents of the students in the school. The Christmas Concert (which was referred to as the Winter Concert as the word 'Christmas' was not allowed in the Kingdom...) included singing, classroom presentations and finally, a visit from Santa Claus. The Santa Claus for this event was a twelve year old boy, dressed in the traditional red suit with white beard and cap, came out onto the stage, greeted the audience and then, with his classmates as elves, passed out small bags of candies and oranges for the children in the audience. As this event was taking place several uniformed policemen and members of the Matawa entered the auditorium through the doors near the back. They had apparently pushed their way through our front gate where one of our security workers was on duty and came straight to the auditorium. As soon as they saw what was happening, they rushed to the front of the auditorium and grabbed the young boy who was portraying Santa. The boy was of course terrified and began to cry; meanwhile, one of the Matawa announced to the audience that they were to leave the auditorium. A mother, who had been filming the concert, turned her camera on the Matawa; he saw her do this and immediately told one of his colleagues to take the camera from her. She protested and the camera was immediately wrested from her and thrown to the floor. The principal, who by this time had come to the front of the auditorium, announced to the parents and teachers that they should leave quietly. He then confronted the policemen and insisted that they leave the premises immediately. They began to walk toward the exits, but were taking the young Santa Claus with them. The principal told them in no uncertain terms that they should not take the young boy, and volunteered to take his place. The police released the boy and took the principal with them. He went through an experience similar to mine; he was held in a locked room in the police station for several hours.

In the meantime, one of the parents contacted a friend who was an international journalist and the story appeared in international newspapers. The Saudi government was bothered by the publicity and wanted it to end. However, the principal was so enraged, that he sat down and wrote a letter to the Director of the Royal Commission denigrating and denouncing the police and their tactics. It was an unwise thing to do. He was told to leave the Kingdom immediately. He was released as principal of the school and completed the balance of his contract (about six months) in the school's district office. This incident continued to raise its ugly head even during the years I worked in the city; no one had ever forgotten it and the Saudis considered it an affront to their religion and culture.

Evening performances for parents were always sensitive. Although our school had the tacit approval of the government and local authorities to function behind our walls as normal western schools, many community officials and even parents of our students had strong ideas about what should and what should not be allowed. This situation created suspicion and mistrust among many officials of the Royal Commission and others who believed that our school and its community should adhere strictly to religious laws. Of course, by virtue of the fact that we had a co-educational student body and faculty, these strict religious laws were already ignored—with the blessing of the government of Saudi Arabia. As principal of the school and therefore the go-between between the school and the community and government, I found myself walking a very thin line on many occasions. I extended on-going invitations to the local education authorities to attend any and all activities sponsored by the school. They rarely took us up on the invitations, but occasionally would drop into the school to observe what was really happening.

United Nations Transgression

One evening, we had a performance for parents during United Nations week, in which students from all classes participated. The auditorium was appropriately decorated with the flags of many nations from around the world. As the show got underway, I was surprised and gratified to see the head of the local department of education enter the auditorium. He had been educated in North America and spoke excellent English. I immediately made my way to the back of the auditorium and invited him to come to the front and sit with me in order that I could later introduce him to the audience. He kindly consented to do so. As the program ended I gave a short laudatory speech during which I introduced this official to the audience. He acknowledged their applause and then, as he and I made our way down the aisle and out of the building, he grabbed my hand and, as was a customary practice in Saudi, held my hand as we walked out. Of course, were the audience local persons only, it would have seemed natural. But because I was western, the spectacle of two grown men holding hands was peculiar to see. It took several weeks for many of the faculty and students to quit talking about that incident. I must admit that I felt somewhat odd holding this official's hand.

A couple of days later I received a notice from the Assistant Head of the Royal Commission to meet in his office. When I arrived in his office, I received a severe reprimand for having had an Israeli flag on display in the school. I was informed that the display of an Israeli flag anywhere in the Kingdom was illegal! Go figure—we held hands and he still ratted me out!

Church Steeples are a No-No

During another evening meeting for parents in my first year, I felt it necessary to admonish parents to abstain from gossiping or listening to gossip regarding the school and its operation. Too many stories circulated throughout the community that were just not true and which contributed to the difficulties the school had existing in the community. I used the example of a person climbing to the top of a tall church steeple on a windy night and releasing the feathers of a pillow and then trying to gather the feathers the next day to demonstrate the difficulties of quelling rumors in a community. The metaphor was fine, except for one thing—there are no church steeples in Saudi Arabia and the concept was lost on most members of the audience. The faculty of the school presented me with the 'golden camel' award for making major gaffs in the community. (The 'golden camel' was a small brass camel imbedded in a base of clear plastic which contained the droppings of a camel and which was circulated from staff member to staff member in recognition of cultural gaffs perpetrated in the school community.)

Crown Prince Visit

When the day of the Crown Prince's visit finally arrived, everyone in the city, including our students, was excited. So much preparation had gone into the rare visit by royalty—new statues and monuments, streets cleaned, buildings built, houses painted, palm trees pruned and washed, new landscaping put in medians in the center of streets and even a new ten kilometer road paved through the desert so he would be able to go to the seaside for lunch. The city was awash with police and security. Several days before his visit, the assistant superintendent called me and indicated that I should come up with three thousand riyals to purchase small flags for our students to wave when the Crown Prince was driven into the city. It seemed like a considerable amount of money for small, plastic flags—we only needed about 250 of them as he also indicated that only our male students should be allowed to stand in the street. Inviting girls to welcome the Crown Prince was not acceptable. One day before the visit, the flags arrived and they were truly cheap; I was convinced that much of the money we had used to purchase these went into someone's pocket. I was not pleased; it is never good to feel as principal of a school where all expenses are covered by tuition that any of the money might be wasted. Nevertheless, there was little that could be done about it. On the long-awaited day, I and most of our other male teachers accompanied our male students out to the road down which the Crown Prince would enter our city. Because the weather is always hot in Saudi Arabia, standing out in the hot sun for an indeterminate amount of time might just prove difficult. Consequently, I ensured that several cases of bottled water were delivered to the location assigned to the 'western' students. We discovered that male students from Saudi schools were located on both sides of us and it didn't take long to discover that they had not been provided with flags or water.

It was nearly two hours later that we began to question the efficacy of bringing our students out to stand in the hot sun. Although we parceled out our water, it was apparent that the heat was beginning to dampen the enthusiasm of our students. The Saudi students standing on either side of us were not supervised; their teachers recognized a bad situation and simply didn't arrive. As we passed water out to our students, it became apparent that the Saudi boys were not happy; eventually they began to push our boys around and take their water bottles. My teachers and I attempted to prevent this from happening, but came under significant verbal abuse—in broken English—and realized that we would have to depart the location to prevent violence. At that moment, a large green bus with silvered windows turned from the highway into our street. There were several police vehicles in front and behind the bus and policemen on motorcycles. The bus flew by us at approximately sixty kilometers per hour, a cloud of sand blowing in our faces; there was nothing to be seen through the tinted windows, not a waving monarch nor even a friendly smile. It was over! We had spent more than a thousand dollars for flags and water, had been abused and sworn at by our Saudi hosts, and had several students sick from too much sun—what a wonderful school day! Needless to say I vowed I would never allow students to leave school again for such an activity.

High School Start-up

When western schools began to operate in the Kingdom in the mid-1950, the Ministry of Education made the decision that only primary, elementary and junior high schools would be allowed status. Consequently, once western students completed Grade 8, either the family left the Kingdom, or, as is the norm in Britain, students were sent abroad to study in boarding schools. Naturally, this created significant family issues for many families, in particular those from North America and India, who were unhappy separating their families by sending their children off at such a young age. Finally, the Ministry of Education lifted the ban on western secondary schools in the Kingdom. I believe the first western high school started up in the city of Jeddah, and shortly thereafter, other schools recognized the value of offering secondary education to their western constituents. As principal of a Kindergarten through Grade 8 school, I had many meetings with our parents, many of whom were highly supportive of creating a high school. Finally, after a number of meetings with the superintendent of our school system, I was given the "go-ahead" to begin a high school. In order to move into high school education as smoothly as possible and, naturally, to defray significant start-up costs, we decided to initiate a gradual move into secondary education. In 2001, we moved sixteen students from Grade 9 into Grade 10 and then, for the next two years, added the next grade level. At the end of the third year these original students received high school diplomas and a high school had been created. I considered the establishment of this secondary school in the Kingdom to be a significant achievement. However, I was not destined to remain in the school as principal.

CHAPTER X

DISTRICT OFFICE ADMINISTRATION

Assistant Superintendent Human Resources

I applied for and was selected to become an assistant superintendent responsible for human resources within our school district. Specifically, my responsibilities encompassed recruitment of 'sponsored' faculty, hiring of 'local' teachers, aides and cleaners, contract disputes, policy revisions, human resources reports for the school board, attendance at myriads of meetings and general support of the superintendent in his activities. Inasmuch as our school district was comprised of ten schools, more than five hundred employees and several diverse and geographically separated locations, the commitments required of me as a school district administrator were enormous. The appointment required a move from our home of four years near the Red Sea to the Arabian Gulf side of the Kingdom in a home on the campus where the district offices were located.

Alcohol and Caning

The drinking of alcohol in Saudi Arabia is forbidden. However, the Kingdom has a long and complex history relating to alcohol abuse, and, once one arrives in the Kingdom, it is obvious that booze is available. Most westerners will claim that nearly from the moment they arrive, alcoholic drinks are offered for consumption. Westerners have become adept at brewing their own wine, beer, and in some cases, pure alcohol. Recipes for brewing a variety of alcoholic drinks were everywhere available and ingredients could be easily purchased in any grocery store. Brewers of pure alcohol which could be used for hard liquor drinks often became wealthy selling their product. Moonshiners seemed to be in every major population center, and once one learned whom to contact, it was possible to buy "siddiqui" (Arabic word for 'friend') for personal, and in some case, even commercial use. Also, again once one met the appropriate people, black market alcohol of any and all varieties was available at a price—a bottle of whiskey would usually cost somewhere in the neighborhood of $120.00.

As assistant superintendent in charge of human resources, many unusual situations became my responsibility to deal with. A young male teacher from South Africa had gotten himself into trouble. The police typically would not hassle westerners for drinking of alcohol as long as it was done out of the view of the public. As one police chief said to me, "We know what you are doing behind the walls of your compounds. As long as people confine themselves to those locations, no one will pursue or punish them for the consumption of alcohol." The unfortunate young teacher had spent the afternoon and evening drinking, and then, under the considerable influence of alcohol decided to accompany some friends to another compound to eat supper in a restaurant located there. When their vehicle pulled up in front of the compound and they climbed out of the car, the teacher stumbled and fell to the ground. Sitting right there in a police car were two Saudi policemen. They saw the young man fall to the ground and went over to him to see if he were hurt. When they realized that he was drunk and nearly incapable of standing, they immediately put him in handcuffs and arrested him. He was taken to a nearby police station and locked up.

In Saudi, when a westerner is placed in jail, the police do not contact anyone. Consequently, it is nearly impossible to find someone who has been arrested for several hours or even days. By the time this young man was located, he had already gone before a judge and been convicted of public drunkenness—the sentence was 79 strokes with a cane. He was placed under house arrest, meaning that he was to stay in his apartment until such time as the punishment could be carried out, and he became my responsibility. Over the next several weeks, I accompanied him to court on two occasions and drove him to a prison three times. The court reaffirmed his sentence and also imposed expulsion from the Kingdom on the fulfillment of the punishment. The first time I took the young man to the prison for the sentence to be carried out, after waiting around in the courtyard for more than an hour, we were sent away. Apparently, in addition to me as a representative of the organization who employed him, a court judge, a lawyer and the man who would do the caning had to all be present. They were unable to find a judge in the prison who would stand still long enough for the sentence to be carried out. In the meantime, the young teacher's work visa had been revoked and he was no longer under contract to our school.

Nearly thirty days passed before the young man was again summoned to the prison for the punishment to be carried out. During this time, I had often provided him with groceries, ensured that he was getting mail from his family and was the one person with whom he could have conversations. As the time of his incarceration increased, he became increasingly despondent and discouraged. He wanted nothing more than to have get over the punishment and fly home. Finally on the day he was again summoned to the prison, I drove to his apartment and picked him up. He was wearing two pairs of jeans and three shirts because he had heard that he would be caned with his clothing on.

Upon arrival in the prison, I drove my vehicle inside the gates and we climbed out of the car. There in front of us was a prison employee in thobe and gutra, carrying a meter-long slender rod of rattan which had a small knob on the taped-handle end. Standing next to him were two elderly Saudi gentlemen introduced as a judge and a lawyer. The man who would carry out the caning immediately told the fellow to stand against the rear of my vehicle and place his hands on the top of the car. We didn't even go inside of the buildings! I had heard that the man performing the caning would be required to place a copy of the Koran under his armpit to keep the strokes from becoming too strong. This was not the case. He immediately placed the cane against the teacher's shoulders and then began the beating. It was quite different from what we had anticipated. Using his wrist as a fulcrum, the strokes landed, almost faster than the eye could follow, from shoulder to buttocks, back and forth. The actual caning took no longer than a minute, and the strokes were lightly landed—with the exception of the final two strokes which were administered with a snap and a loud noise. They hurt. The judge then announced the punishment had been completed, only 79 strokes because the man was an infidel and didn't deserve to receive the 80 strokes that the Koran proscribed. With that, we were instructed to get back in our car and leave the prison. It was with a great deal of relief and a lifting of stress that I was able to put the young man on an airplane the next day. He flew out of the Kingdom and would never again return.

It is my belief that this young man was punished in the manner described because he was not Caucasian. He was from South Africa and had a darker skin. I do not believe that if he had been a white person he would have received the same punishment, as over the eight years I was in Saudi Arabia, I saw others in trouble with the police for a variety of transgressions and none of them were humiliated in the same manner.

Cultural and Racial Bias

Unfortunately, it was not unusual to see discriminatory practices in the Kingdom. Because of the large number of labourers--usually third world nationals, present in the Kingdom, abuses are common. Despite efforts to replace foreigners with Saudis, the Kingdom remains highly dependent on foreign labour. Nearly two-thirds of all jobs are still held by foreigners.

Saudi men simply do not work in what would be considered menial, labor positions. All physical labor in the country is carried out by the foreign work force—more than six million men and women. These persons, usually arriving in the Kingdom with no expertise and no training, commonly work fourteen to fifteen hour days, live in dirty hovels and are abused physically and verbally by their Saudi employers. Women are typically brought into homes as cooks, cleaners and babysitters. They too are often treated as 'modern slaves'. Foreigners cannot work in the Kingdom without a Saudi sponsor, who typically provides accommodations and pays travel expenses, including a trip home every couple of years. Usually, the sponsor holds the employee's passport and an employee cannot leave the country or change jobs without the sponsor's permission.

The school had hired two Americans, a husband and wife teaching couple, both of whom had grown up in the United States although their families were originally from Asia. Both had been educated and trained in North America. The discrimination evident in the Kingdom was amply illustrated on the occasion when they arrived back in the Kingdom after having vacationed in Asia. As they disembarked from the airplane in Jeddah, the woman was rudely grabbed and forced to join a line of Asian women arriving as workers. When she protested that she was a teacher, working in the Kingdom at a western school and in possession of a bona-fide teacher's work permit, the official slapped her face and told her to get back in line and to be silent. When this incident came to my attention, I initiated a meeting with immigration authorities to complain and to try to do something about it. After several meetings and official letters, eventually we were able to procure an official letter for the teacher to carry in her passport which described her circumstances in the Kingdom and which was signed by the Minister in charge of immigration. In the future she was always able to produce this letter, but it certainly didn't stop the bad looks and verbal ranting that often accompanied her wherever she was in the Kingdom.

Demonstration Against the West

For nurses, engineers, teachers and other professionals from countries like the United States or Great Britain, working in Saudi Arabia can be extremely lucrative and surprisingly pleasant. Most Westerners live in walled compounds with swimming pools, tennis courts, attractive landscaping and well-stocked commissaries. There are no taxes and gasoline costs less than $.30 per litre. With the companies paying the rent, utilities, international school tuitions, health care and even providing round trip air tickets once per year to visit home, life could not be much better.

One Friday afternoon, which was part of the weekend in Saudi (because their religion determined Friday to be the holy day of the week, all businesses and schools were off on Thursday and Friday which constituted their weekend), I was working in my office at the district office. The superintendent was also working that day as was his habit and in the early afternoon called me to come to his office on the second floor. He stated that he had been hearing peculiar noises coming from outside of the building and wondered if I had heard the same. I hurried up the stairs to his office and we moved to the other side of the building to look outside. Our district offices were located in a relatively new building on the same campus as three of our schools. This campus was situated right next door to the United States Consulate for the eastern part of the Kingdom and was completely surrounded by a three meter wall. When we looked out the window and over the wall toward the entry to the compounds, we were startled to see hundreds of Saudi men milling about on the highway in front of the entrance. They were chanting and holding up signs written in Arabic. The chanting seemed to be various versions of "Americans go home!" The highway was completely blocked by vehicles which had simply been stopped and left standing in the middle of the road, effectively blocking all traffic. As we observed these events, we noticed that there appeared to be some ring leaders—that is, men who were organizing the shouting and who seemed to be at the middle of the crowds. These men were generally bearded, wearing short thobes and gutras without igal—Matawa. Suddenly from the south, a large line of policemen, all wearing their "riot gear" and brandishing clubs, moved into position between the rioters and the entrance to the consulate compound. They carried shields and immediately locked arms in a show of force. The rioters continued to yell and to mill about and paid little attention to the policemen.

I learned later that several years earlier, there had been a similar riot and that the Saudis had actually breached the compound and wandered through the buildings causing minor damage and disruption. In those days, there was not a high wall in evidence completely surrounding the compounds, nor was there a fifty calibre machine gun at the entrance. These enhancements had all come in later years.

As the rioters continued to demonstrate their dissatisfaction with the United States, it became evident that they had come directly from prayers at the mosques—and that the riot was an organized event. Demonstrators of all ages were in evidence, from the very old to the very young; many of the rioters had brought their young sons along to participate. Finally, after more than an hour, the policemen began to move forward, herding the demonstrators before them. As they approached the front ranks, they began to swing their clubs indiscriminately around them. I observed many of the rioters being hit. It took the police nearly an hour to move the rioters away from the scene. We later learned that several of the 'ring leaders' had been arrested and taken to the prison. It was not until after dark that evening that all of the abandoned vehicles had been driven or hauled from the highway.

Apparently, the imams had challenged the true believers to demonstrate in front of the US Consulate that afternoon after prayers to indicate that they were not supporting the United States in its aggressive war in Iraq. To us, educators living in the Kingdom, this riot was the harbinger of difficult times coming. The whole complexion of living in the Kingdom would take on a completely different look in the coming months and years.

The superintendent resigned his position shortly after this incident to become the director of another international school in the Kingdom. As his resignation was fairly abrupt, I was the logical candidate to be appointed superintendent of schools as his replacement.

Security in the Kingdom

In the weeks and months following these incidents, security in the Kingdom became a major consideration. Every housing compound, business, school and institution found it necessary to begin planning for security in case of terrorist attack. As principal, I had spent more than a year and a half supervising the construction of an even higher wall around my school. What had been a two-meter high wall became a three-meter wall. Police were assigned full-time posts outside of the walls in the parking lots. The compounds in which westerners lived became difficult to enter. No longer could one simply drive to the gate, indicate to the workers where one intended to go, and drive in. All vehicles were now required to stop, to undergo searches for weapons, bombs, and what have you, as well as for all drivers and passengers to provide valid, up-to-date identification before entry was allowed. The entrances to compounds received significant defensive upgrading, from speed bumps, drop gates, chicanes and heavily armed guards to heavy mobile machine guns. No one was allowed simply to approach a gate, identify oneself and drive in. Needless to say, living in the Kingdom was becoming much more difficult, uncomfortable and unpleasant.

Western schools were considered by many to be vulnerable targets. While most experts did not believe that schools full of children would come under violent attack, nevertheless it occurred to most that the children of important western engineers, business men and CEO's could become valid terror objectives. Consequently, security and safety planning became a significant responsibility of school administrators. Parents, students and faculty members became increasingly nervous and apprehensive as living and working conditions in the Kingdom deteriorated relative to safety and security. Many hours were spent discussing, planning and putting new security procedures into effect. Of course, construction of safety barriers, whether human or concrete, was costly. School budgets had never been based on these expenses, and, although they were real and significant, companies and parents who were responsible for tuitions would not tolerate significant increases to their costs. Consequently, school programs, facility improvements and even employee remunerations suffered as a direct result of the increasing insecurity of the Middle East.

Attack at School

Early in May, 2004, I, then superintendent of the school district, was in my office early in the morning getting an early start on the day. The telephone began to ring, and because there were as yet no secretaries in the building, I answered it. The call was coming from the principal of the school located nearly a thousand miles away on the west coast of Saudi Arabia. He said in an emotional and tremulous voice, "Fred. We are under attack! There are terrorists outside of the wall shooting at our compound!" I asked him to slow down and asked, "Where are you? Are you at school?" He replied, "No, we're at home. My wife and I have locked ourselves here in the second floor bathroom and are hunkering down. We don't know what else to do! Here, listen! You can hear the gunfire!" In the background I could definitely hear the sputtering of machine guns and the loud, singular reports of rifle fire. We remained on the telephone for about ten minutes, and then, because the frequency of gunfire had lessened, I suggested that he call the other faculty members living in the compound and tell them to sequester themselves in their homes and to remain there until safety was assured. He and I agreed to call all faculty members living in his city and instruct to them that they remain in their homes for the day. After nearly thirty minutes, he telephoned me again; we had reached all of the teachers but one and had instructed all of them to remain in their houses. At this point, the gunfire was no longer evident; at least, we could no longer hear any explosions. I informed him that I would book air passage and be there with him the following day.

Here is what happened that day. Early that morning, three Saudi employees of a western oil subsidiary company had entered the office complex as was their daily routine. They were trusted employees, spoke excellent English and had worked there for several years. After gaining entry, these three, (it was reported they were two brothers and a cousin), opened an emergency gate and allowed a fourth conspirator into the compound. He carried with him weapons with which they armed themselves and then entered the offices. They walked slowly through the company offices, shooting whomever they encountered. Shortly, two Americans, two Britons, and an Australian lay dead. Three others, an American, a Pakistani and a Canadian were wounded. The perpetrators then left the building, carrying the body of an American to their white pick-up truck. They tied this body to the back bumper of the vehicle and then headed from the industrial area where the office was located into the urban section of the city.

The street they followed ran past the McDonald's restaurant (the only western restaurant in the city); they fired several bullets at the building resulting in damage to the exterior. They continued down this main thoroughfare which happened to pass directly in front of our western school. Pulling into the parking lot, they were surprised to encounter policemen stationed near the entrance to the school. Nevertheless, they threw a pipe bomb over the wall which exploded near the main entrance to the school. A cleaner, having heard the noise, and who had come outside to investigate, was wounded slightly by a flying fragment from the bomb. Two teachers, a husband and wife (those that we had not been able to reach by telephone) were already in the school and working in the teachers' workroom. They heard the explosion, and shortly thereafter gunfire, and hit the floor. They remained on the floor near the photocopy machine for the next several minutes.

The police in the parking lot began to fire their weapons at the four terrorists in their truck. The terrorists made a u-turn in the parking lot and then pulled out onto the street in front of the school. They returned fire as they drove past the policemen; three of the bullets hit the external wall of the school just under the eaves causing slight damage. Leaving the area, the pick-up drove down the street, through an intersection and then directly past a Saudi boys' high school on the next block. It appears they wanted to show off their activities to the Saudi students who were beginning to arrive at that school. Speculation has it that at least two of the terrorists had graduated from that high school and they were hoping to not only 'show off', but to elicit sympathy and support from the young men at the school. They turned their vehicle around and headed back in the direction from which they had come. Once again the terrorists made a u-turn in front of our school and exchanged fire with the policemen stationed there.

The terrorists drove into the intersection between the schools and made a right turn. They drove about a block down the street where they encountered a young Saudi in an official vehicle belonging to a Saudi government organization. They stopped the vehicle, sent the driver packing, abandoned their white pick-up and hijacked the official vehicle. They halted another vehicle, driven by a Saudi citizen, and commandeered it as well. The two vehicles headed for the highway which joined the industrial city with the old city. The distance between the two city sections being approximately ten kilometres, they sped down the highway heading into the city. On the outskirts of the old city, they turned off the highway and headed for the one western business in the area—the Holiday Inn. The Holiday Inn was located right next to the western compound in which resided the majority of our western teachers.

Pulling into the parking area in front of the hotel, the terrorists once again opened fire with their weapons. Of course, because of the heightened security measures in the country, there were armed guards located in this compound as well. The terrorists again came under return fire. They drove out of the parking lot in front of the hotel, turned right and headed for the western compound where our teachers were just getting ready to drive to school. As they neared the front entrance, national guardsmen who were stationed in front of the compound opened fire on the terrorists with a machine gun and rifles. (This was of course the gunfire that the principal called me about and which I was able to hear over the telephone.) The gunfire was significant and the terrorist shortly gave up their attempt to enter the compound, turned their vehicle around and headed back toward the highway and the old city. (Minutes later, a western expat, attempting to get home to the compound to ensure that his family was safe, came under fire from the guardsmen—they not realizing he wasn't one of the terrorists. His car was hit and immediately caught on fire. It burned and was destroyed just in front of the entrance to the compound. He was able to escape the burning vehicle and the gunfire safely.)

As the attack had now been going on for nearly an hour, the security forces, police and National Guard were alerted and hunting for the terrorists had begun in earnest. As the terrorists drove into the old city, they were accosted at several points, shots were exchanged and eventually all of the terrorists were shot. Three of them died during the gun battles and the fourth died a short time later from his injuries. In addition to the five expatriates mentioned above, one Saudi National Guard soldier was killed, eight national guardsmen were wounded, as were a further ten public security personnel. The incident ended approximately ninety minutes after it began.

I arrived in the city the next morning on the first available flight. I immediately attended a public meeting held at the western compound during which the United States Consul spoke. He talked of the gravity of the situation for western expatriates in the Kingdom and suggested that the terrorists, even though they were dead, had accomplished their purpose—to terrorize and frighten westerners in the Kingdom. He was proven to be correct in that more than thirty percent of western expatriate employees and their families left the Kingdom within thirty days.

That afternoon I held a meeting with our teachers; all teachers, overseas hires as well as local hires, attended the meeting. This particular meeting was perhaps the most difficult meeting of my educational career. Of course, I was in constant contact with the chairman of our school board, a Briton who worked for a British aerospace company, and he gave me permission to do whatever I believed I had to do in order to retain our teachers in the Kingdom long enough to complete the school year. I went into the meeting with the intention of maintaining as many teachers as possible in order to keep out school in operation. Although our over-seas hired teachers made up about sixty percent of our teaching faculty, the student population of the school was predominantly local—that is, they were the children of workers in the Kingdom who had more or less permanent residency. They would not be leaving the Kingdom—terrorist attacks or not. Prior to the meeting, I asked all of the teachers to write out their thoughts, feelings and experiences and to submit them to me in order that I could understand what they were thinking and what their plans might be. Interestingly, these two and three page reports, while accounting the terror and fears they felt in their homes, generally indicated that they would prefer seeing the school year brought to a professional end. In the meeting, I presented to the teachers the options of leaving without penalty, of sending out family members but remaining to complete the school year and of remaining to complete a shortened school year with an added financial incentive. Locally hired teachers and staff would benefit from the financial incentive.

After the meeting was complete, I insisted that teachers be ready to give me their decision the following day. The school would remain closed for three days, and then, with their compliance, would open again for three weeks. This would necessitate the shortening of two weeks of school, but final exams, marks and completed lessons would be the result. This would appease tuition-paying parents and companies. The next day I spoke with all members of the teaching staff and received their decisions. I was gratified to recognize, that with the exception of one teacher, all would remain to complete the school year. The professionalism inherent in that decision was amazing; after all that had happened I was tremendously impressed with the teachers who made that decision. I was so pleased to be able to announce to parents that their children would not lose out on their school year.

When I called the board chairman and explained to him the options I had given to the teachers and the decisions that they had made, he told me that he would have to have the board meet in an emergency meeting to allow additional monies to be paid in the form of bonuses. A quickly-called board meeting was held and to professional consternation but eventual relief, all but one member of the board supported my decisions and we were able to keep the school open and operating. The one dissenting board member was the chairman of the finance committee. Oh, well.

The school year ended in three weeks; all of the overseas hired teachers took their families and returned home for the summer holidays and all were safe. When the next school year began at the end of the summer, only two teaching families did not return to the Kingdom.

Attack at the Petroleum Center

Unfortunately, this was not the end of the terrorist attacks in the Kingdom that year which affected the operation of our schools. On the 29th of May, in the city of Khobar, located on the east coast, terrorists attacked two sites related to the oil industry. Early in the morning, at approximately 6:45 a.m., four terrorists in a vehicle approached an office complex which housed several offices associated with the oil industry. They attempted to enter the complex through the front gates, shooting at guards and employees who were nearby. At the time of their attack, an American employee also arrived at the gate where he and two of his co-workers were shot and killed. At least two of the terrorists entered the building and moved through several offices looking for targets.

One of our school board members, in fact, as coincidence would have it, the only board member who had disagreed with my handling of the affair on the western coast just four weeks earlier, was working in the building. He told me that as soon as they heard the initial gunshots as the terrorists approached the front gates, he and the other workers who were in the building (it was early and regular hours had not yet commenced) vacated the offices. As the area was surrounded by a high wall, they could not escape the grounds. Instead, they made their way through the four story building to the roof. On the roof they moved as far as possible away from the doorway and hid themselves behind the several large air conditioning units located there. He told me that after several minutes, they heard the door open and a terrorist came out onto the roof looking for victims. Apparently, seeing no one and without walking to the far side of the roof, he re-entered the building. (This information was given me in a telephone conversation about a week after the incident took place; this board member apologized to me for having not supported me in my difficult decisions, and then resigned his position on the board. I never saw the man again.) More firing came from the street below. Police had arrived and were engaged in a gun battle with two of the gunmen. They were shot and killed in short order and a third gunman was killed as he ran from the building. The fourth terrorist was able to escape over the wall into an adjoining housing compound, where he stole a vehicle and left the area.

At nearly the same time, approximately 7:15 a.m., another group of terrorists in another vehicle attacked a housing compound rented to an oil company subsidiary group. This housing compound was inhabited by foreigners working in Saudi Arabia, and, coincidently was the home of one of our teachers in our high school whose husband was employed by that company. When they arrived, they fired an RPG at the guardhouse, killing the two security guards inside. A school bus had just picked up children to take them to school and was attempting to leave the gate. They shot at the bus and killed a ten year old boy. A high-ranking employee of the company, who had shortly before dropped his wife off at our school (she was not a teacher but was accompanying a group of our students on a fieldtrip to another city), also entered the compound as the attack was occurring. His car came under attack and he was wounded; the terrorists pulled him out of the vehicle, still alive. Taking a page out of the attack on the west coast earlier that month, they tied this Briton to the back bumper of their four wheel drive vehicle and drove out onto the highway. However, as they approached the first intersection, a Saudi citizen drove his car into their vehicle and forced them off the roadway. The terrorists immediately shot the Saudi and killed him. The police arrived and, after a short gun battle, killed the terrorists before they could make their escape. The Briton was by this time dead and his facial features had been so destroyed that he was unrecognizable.

While this attack was happening, I had had telephone calls from the security section of the U.S. Consulate informing me of events. I immediately ordered at lock-down at all of our school sites, the majority of our students having just arrived for the school day. Informed that we had a bus on the highway heading north, I ordered the principal to telephone the driver (all of our bus drivers carried a school-owned cell phone reserved for emergencies) and have the bus returned to the school. In the meantime, I learned that the wife of one of the victims (in fact, the very man who was tied to the back of the Saudi vehicle and dragged until he was dead) was acting as a chaperone on that bus. I told the principal to have her escorted to my office when she arrived back at the school. Although we did not know if the information was reliable, I was aware that her husband may have been killed. I called my wife, a counsellor at the high school, explained the situation to her and asked her to come to my office to be with the woman. When they had both arrived, we met in my office and discussed the situation. The wife was highly agitated, and wanted only to have her driver take her home to her compound, which was the one that had been attacked earlier that morning. We told her that, because of the on-going attacks across the city, she would not be allowed to go home. For the next several hours we attempted to get confirming information regarding the status of her husband, but were unable to do so as the police would not give out information—and, as we found out later, because of the condition of her husband's corpse, they had not been able to identify him with certainty. Later that afternoon, when the lock-down was lifted, she was able to return home—only to find that her husband had indeed been cruelly murdered.

Attack at Housing Compound

On the same morning, a third terrorist attack was carried out at a well-known western housing compound located just a short distance from our school. At 7:30 a.m., six terrorists climbed the wall of the compound and, at the same time, five additional terrorist drove up to the security gate. The guards at this compound demanded that a car stop, be checked, and then pull ahead to a second check-point in front of a second gate. On this morning, the second gate was left open, so the vehicle carrying terrorists was able to drive straight through the second gate. One of the terrorists stood up in the sunroof of their vehicle and machine gunned the two armed guards at the gate. A school bus was behind the terrorist vehicle and he then turned his weapon on the school bus, opened fire and killed two children and wounded four others. As the vehicle carrying the terrorists moved ahead into the compound, a security guard ushered the rest of the children off of the bus and led them to a safer area in the compound.

The terrorists joined forces in the compound with their colleagues who had scaled the walls and then began to move methodically through the residential complex. They kicked in the doors of the residences, asked the inhabitants whether they were Muslims. If they answered in the negative, they were to be killed. Some had their throats slit in their residence; others were escorted to the compound's Italian restaurant. (The restaurant was very well known among other westerners in the city because of its extensive menu and excellent food; my wife and I had eaten there on more than one occasion.) In the restaurant, the terrorists murdered an Italian cook and a Swedish chef, both of whom were beheaded. They also killed an American and several others; it was reported later that most of these were shot in the head.

During that day, the terrorists moved through that section of the large compound with impunity. However, because it was separated from other parts of the compound by walls, they remained only in that area. I received a telephone call from friends whose children attended our school and who lived in one of the other sections; they were hunkered down in their apartment, doors locked, lights out and furniture piled in front of the doors. They were calling to check on the status of their son who had stayed at my home the previous night. My son and he were very close friends and often slept over at one another's homes.

Several students who attended our schools lived in that compound. The principal of our elementary school had several calls from families who were sequestered in their homes, fearing for their lives. One child in particular called several times during the day and whispered that she was hiding with her grandparents in their washroom.

An American woman who worked as a substitute teacher in our schools lived on that compound. Shortly after it was attacked, she heard someone kicking at her front door. Determined to leave the compound, she went to her back door. Holding her breath, she began running. Immediately she heard rifle blasts right behind her and suddenly realized she was the target! Looking over her shoulder, she saw a young man, no more than twenty years old, shooting at her. As the bullets buzzed and sang around her, she suddenly fell to the pavement. A bullet had caught her in the back of her leg. As she lay there bleeding, she turned to the young terrorist and scolded him for shooting her. She looked away, anticipating the worst, and, then, when nothing happened, looked back. He was no longer there. She was able to crawl slowly away and eventually was rescued and her wound treated.

By this time, the compound had been surrounded by Saudi Emergency Forces and the international press; the forces established telephone contact with the terrorists and began to negotiate for their surrender. It appeared impossible for the terrorists to make any escape. They however then took fifty-four people hostage and sent them to the sixth floor of the hotel which was situated in the eastern end of the compound. They placed explosives at the entrance to the hotel and vowed to kill the hostages if they were not allowed to leave. During the confusion, at least three terrorists were able to climb over the wall, steal a car and escape. At approximately 2130 that evening, Saudi Emergency Forces were able to gain entrance to the underground parking garage where the surviving children from the school bus were hiding and moved them out of the compound. Some British nursery school workers were also rescued at this time.

During this same day, it was reported that a vehicle containing four armed men was driving around from compound to compound shooting guards—at least eleven were injured at five other housing compounds.

The next morning, the terrorists ate breakfast in the restaurant where they had murdered several people the day before. They made the decision to kill all Hindus in the compound and killed eight Indian nationals in the next few minutes. They continued to negotiate with the Saudi forces for their release. The negotiations went on most of the day, with sporadic gunfire and explosions being heard across the city.

By this time, everyone in the city knew that the incident was happening and were staying in their homes. We cancelled school at all of our sites.

At approximately 2:00 a.m. the next morning, Saudi forces attempted to enter the hotel where the hostages were being kept. Several police were injured by two explosions and the terrorists demanded the rest pull back or the remaining hostages would all be killed. Two American military men were also injured at this time and were later flown out of the Kingdom to Kuwait.

I had not gone to bed that night at all; like most westerners in the Kingdom, I remained awake listening to the news in order to understand what was happening. Early in the morning, as the sun was beginning to come up, I heard helicopters flying directly over my house. I went out onto my back patio and saw four large helicopters heading for the top of the hotel in the compound. From where I stood, I could see the soldiers sliding down ropes from the helicopters to the roof of the hotel. Significant gunfire was heard at this time, and it turned out that the firing was a diversion by ground forces to distract the terrorists from the helicopter troops. (That morning, one of the consulate workers showed me a fifty calibre machine gun bullet which had landed on the grass in front of his house.) Shortly after the helicopters left, Saudi authorities announced that the hostages in the hotel and compound were free and that the terrorists had either been killed or captured. It later turned out that only two were killed and one captured—the majority had fled unimpeded before the raid took place. There was a great deal of controversy regarding what had actually happened; how had these men escaped an area that was completely surrounded? Saudi authorities never answered that question and most believe that some type of deal had been struck to allow them to leave unimpeded.

After these attacks, the situation in Saudi Arabia for westerners was considered exceedingly dangerous. Consequently, many foreign workers, including a small number of our teachers, fled the country and didn't return as they considered it too dangerous to stay. Many of the western companies moved their employees to surrounding Middle Eastern countries and carried on their work from afar. It is notable that many westerners, even after this, decided to remain in the Kingdom and go about their lives. Obviously, the impact on our schools was significant; we lost nearly a third of our overall student populations and down-sized our operation considerably. World oil prices reacted to these attacks by moving quickly upward.

However, it must be said, that the Saudi security forces did a good job. For the next several months, they were able to find and capture or kill a large number of terrorists. And the terrorists were not able to significantly neither damage the oil facilities nor interrupt the manufacture and exportation of oil products out of the Kingdom. Security was beefed up and life became less enjoyable; it became nearly impossible for Westerners to move around the cities and deserts. Many students and teachers left the Kingdom—and who could blame them?

During this time, as superintendent in charge of the safety and security of more than two thousand students and nearly five hundred employees, the stresses and pressures of the job were significant. At no time during my years of preparation for leadership had anyone prepared me for dealing with such difficult possibilities. University courses did not even mention such things as terrorists, automatic weapons, violent attacks on children and teachers or even security measures that should be followed to obviate against such occurrences. Consequently, on-the-job training was necessary. I became a member of a security committee, headed up by oil-related companies and, at least partially, by the U.S. Consulate, to become informed of methods, strategies and preventative measures that could be possibly taken.

Even though three of our schools and our district office were located on property adjacent to the U. S. Consulate on the eastern coast of the Kingdom and had, consequently a two meter wall completely surrounding the property, security experts suggested to me that an even higher wall should be erected and closed circuit television cameras should be installed. Fortunately, because our school district was recognized by the United States Government as a necessity for providing western education in the Middle East, it also qualified for government security grants. At any rate, we embarked on a significant building project to bolster the safety for our students and teachers. Once again, I was engaged in the construction of a wall for added security—a costly and time-consuming project. Naturally, because this enhancement of security was undertaken at one location, it was necessary to plan and increase security arrangements at all of our other school sites. Even though I had never studied nor concerned myself with such security concerns, I spent many hundreds of hours working towards increased security for our schools.

School Closures

At about the same time as these issues were percolating, another of our schools on the other side of the Kingdom experienced a terrorist episode. One morning, as students were being bussed into a compound where we had had a school for more than ten years, a gunman opened fire on the compound with a high-powered rifle. Although he did not injure anyone, possibly because he was a significant distance away and was sniping with a rifle, nevertheless, the consequences were far-reaching. Shortly after this incident, the Saudi heads of the compound where the school was located called me to a meeting. At this meeting I was informed that the parents of children in the school and the heads of the companies supporting the school had determined to find new management for the school. Although they suggested that it had nothing to do with the recent terrorist episode, nevertheless, our organization would no longer be involved. This of course was a difficult situation for the superintendent of schools, but one that had to be met with diplomacy and care. After a number of meetings, I had the unfortunate experience of ending our association with the school—much to the dismay of many of the parents. All of the improvements and equipment (from library books and resources to musical instruments and computers) which our organization had purchased and installed over many years were forfeited, by contract, to the new administrators of the school. Later, I learned that the new managers were in fact a well-known educational organization based in Egypt. They had apparently insinuated themselves into the compound and the school with promises of lower tuitions and better (?) education.

The unstable climate in the Kingdom led to another school closure. Our organization entered into a commitment—the first of its kind—with a private business to manage a western school on a compound located on the southeast coast. Because the business was very large and specialized and consequently hired a significant number of westerners, they wished to open a western-style school for their employees. Our contract, negotiated by my predecessor, required that we provide materials (computers, classroom furniture, sports and music equipment) as well as curricula and textbooks and that we hire and supervise teachers and other school personnel. The business would build the school buildings and provide the play areas. Once again, because of the difficulties politically in Kingdom, the western families began leaving the compound shortly after the opening of the school. Although we fulfilled our financial and managerial obligations, the resulting erosion of western students spelled the end of the need for western-style education. The business decided that 'expensive' western education was not necessary for this particular school, and, once again, by virtue of the contract, we had donated significant valuable materials to a school which we would no longer operate. As superintendent, I attended several meetings and dealt with numerous problems which allowed for us to disassociate ourselves from this school. Again, not an easy situation as there were many parents and students very upset by the circumstances. Stresses caused by meetings with parents, students and company officials were significant and kept me and my colleagues awake in the night.

Government Interference

The government of Saudi was not averse to creating problems for western schools. After they had allowed western secondary schools in the Kingdom, there seemed to be a faction of bureaucrats who did not agree with the decision. Obviously, high schools brought other issues into the Kingdom—western high school students wanted and needed to have access to competitive sports, student government, and worst of all, relationships between males and females. As open relationships between boys and girls were not allowed in the Kingdom for Saudis, co-ed classrooms, dances, and other public displays of affection among western students in western high schools created serious concerns for Saudi officialdom. Even though interactions between western boys and girls were not allowed in public, nevertheless, many officials were not happy.

Our high school on the eastern coast of Saudi had also been created in 2001. It immediately became a successful and populous high school, as students graduating Grade 8 in the large school district of ARAMCO (Saudi Arabian Oil Company) located on the east coast were no longer required to leave home to attend high school. They were able to live with their families and transfer to our high school. Naturally, this was a symbiotic relationship that functioned positively for all parties concerned. But, because older students were now staying at home with their families in the ARAMCO housing compounds, some Saudi officials were not pleased. Finally, after four years of high school in the eastern province, the Ministry of Education came out with a directive indicating, with no stated rationale, that students leaving Grade 8 at ARAMCO would no longer be allowed to transfer to the western high school on our campus. Obviously, dissenting figures in the government and quite probably in the administrative offices of ARAMCO decided that they would put an end to some of the problems that had arisen because of older students remaining in the Kingdom and in the compounds because of access to a western high school. The potential loss of more than sixty percent of our high school students would spell the end of our highly successful high school. The financial obligations of operating a high school would eventually raise the costs of tuition beyond the abilities of parents and companies to pay. The future of our secondary program dimmed.

Our school's contact with the Ministry of Education was mainly facilitated through the office of our assistant superintendent for government relations. This was the same man whom I had worked closely with when living on the western side of the Kingdom. He was a Saudi citizen who had been working for the school district and the superintendent's office for many years. He had built up a significant cadre of contacts at every government level in the Kingdom—including in the Ministry of Education. When the announcement was made that only eight months of ARAMCO student participation in our secondary schools remained, he and I met early in that school year to discuss his goals for the year. I told him that he had only one major goal—facilitate the cancellation of the Ministry's directive regarding students transferring from ARAMCO schools to our high school.

This would be no easy task as very powerful men were instrumental in the creation of the directive. To his credit, he went to work on the problem early in that school year. He spent a significant amount of time meeting with various members of the government and was, eventually, able to set up a meeting between me and the Minister of Education. This was to be the first time that any superintendent of our schools would have the opportunity for a face-to-face meeting with the Minister. Obviously apprehensive, I traveled with my assistant to Riyadh to meet in the government offices. My assistant coached me on how to act and what to say when in the presence of this powerful man. The meeting was somehow anticlimactic; after waiting in a series of offices in the Ministry of Education building, I was eventually ushered into the Minister's office. He sat behind a large mahogany desk, wearing a white gutra and a gold trimmed brown robe over his thobe. He was accompanied by several other men, obviously important in the field of education and specifically with western schools in the Kingdom. The meeting was held in Arabic and, as was usual, translators were present. The meeting was short; after a few pleasant exchanges and questions, I was able to come directly to the point of our concern. I suggested that our school was being unfairly treated because the directive regarding the ban of ARAMCO students in our school would lead to the financial collapse of our program. The Minister listened attentively, and then, through the translator, asked questions which implied that he was completely unaware of the situation and its circumstances. The meeting quickly drew to a close and we were ushered out of the presence of this important gentleman.

I was unsure how successful the meeting was. It was several months before any more information crossed my desk from the Ministry regarding the situation. Finally, I received word that an emissary from the Minister's office wished to visit me on our campus. My assistant assured me that this was an important meeting; he suggested that the man who would visit was the second most important official in the Ministry of Education and that he was favourably disposed to western education in the Kingdom. During our meeting in my office, this gentleman asked many questions, made significant statements regarding our programs and facilities, and then, with an exaggerated facial expression, told me that we had nothing to worry about. He would see to it that the directive, which had been a mutual decision made between bureaucrats and ARAMCO officials, would be reversed. However, he asked me not to divulge any information to anyone regarding this decision until it was officially announced from his office. Apparently, the reversal of the decision was a very political decision and had the potential of creating significant problems within the government. Needless to say, I did not divulge any information. In fact, although I had several meetings with parents of ARAMCO students and officials from their offices, I had to keep silent on the potential outcome. Many of these meetings were emotional and stressful because the parents of the potentially effected students were significantly upset. In fact, the last official meeting that I engaged in as superintendent was with these ARAMCO parents. I had received that day an official letter from the Ministry of Education indicating that ARAMCO students would be able to attend our high school in the future. The directive had been rescinded. This single decision saved our high school and ensured that the school district would have a viable program for many years to come.

Supervision and Evaluation

Perhaps the most onerous and demanding jobs facing school administrators everywhere in the world are the supervision of instruction and the evaluation of teachers. All teachers must be supervised and evaluated. The product of schools is a quality education for the students who pass through the doors. High quality education can only be ensured as long as there is effective 'quality control' in classrooms. Teaching is not an innate skill which anyone can do; contrary to what many persons believe, effective teaching requires technical skills, innovation, dedication and, above all, the ability to communicate with all personality types. Students come in a wide variety of personalities and backgrounds;

a teacher must be able to cope with all types of people and function effectively in every conceivable circumstance. Communicating with all students at the same level of effectiveness is impossible. All good teachers recognize that they must adjust delivery techniques, activities and classroom practices for a wide gamut of receivers...that is, for the extremely varied students who populate schools. And, even then, they realize that they will not reach every student in the very best possible manner for superior results. But teachers must try.

Therein lay the challenges of supervision. Administrators must have the background and perceptions that will allow them to recognize effective teaching in all subjects and in all classrooms. Without these skills, supervision of instruction can deteriorate into nothing but social interactions between teachers and administrators. The goal is, of course, continual and significant improvement in student learning. This is one of those 'easy to say' concepts, but is difficult to actualize. Building a brick wall or digging a ditch are areas which can easily be supervised and evaluated; improving student learning cannot.

Over the years, I was involved with a large variety of supervision practices. Clinical supervision, anecdotal comments, general classroom observations, pre- and post-conferencing, objective-based education, professional discussions and even, what I used to term, "Polaroid snapshots" are some of the wide range of supervision techniques I had employed. (Polaroid snapshots were brief visits to classrooms on a daily basis which provided snapshots of teaching practices; when I was blessed with assistant principals, I insisted that each and every classroom would be visited at least once every day.) It became apparent to me that no one method was the panacea to effective supervision. Because all teachers are different--different backgrounds, different education, different personalities, different teaching areas, different perceptions, different communication skills and practices—well, you get the idea, it is impossible to isolate the most effective supervision method. It is probably for these reasons that many administrators had a difficult time ensuring that effective supervision of instruction was carried on in every classroom.

Of course, supervision of instruction resulted in the practice of teacher evaluation. All teachers, in the schools where I had been involved, were evaluated at the end of every school year. These records were filed in the teacher's personnel file and were generally never again referred to. A perception widely held was that the evaluations were a waste of time. However, nothing is further from the truth. Evaluation files were often referred to in cases of teacher dismissal, litigation, teacher promotion and transfers. Without consistent evaluation references, it would be nearly impossible to accomplish such tasks with efficacy. In international schools, it is common for teachers to fulfill contracts (usually two or three years) and then to move on. Many international teachers want to see and experience as much of the world as they can and find that moving from school to school enables them to do just that; it also broadens their personal education and enhances their teaching. Others find that moving on occasionally, prevents the so-called "burn-out" syndrome from which so many teachers claim to suffer.

Evaluation is, therefore, a significant requirement of the effective administrator's role. The process is time-consuming, and like supervision of instruction, fairly subjective and difficult to complete with professional competence every time. Administrators sometimes dream of 'digging that ditch' so that they could just once see the efficacy of their work.

THE END OF A CAREER

Culminating Events

When I became superintendent in Saudi Arabia, one of my first tasks was to peruse the evaluation files of the seven principals who were working in the district's schools. It was the superintendent's responsibility to evaluate all principals, directors and senior level administrators in the district. Obviously, I wanted to benefit from my predecessor's labours in this regard and to get an impression of the strengths and weaknesses of these persons. In order to be an effective superintendent, which required that I work with these persons and help them to improve their performances, it would be necessary for me to recognize what administrative issues these men and women might have. As I greatly admired and professionally accepted the efforts of the previous superintendent, these evaluation files were valuable to me.

Unfortunately, one of these principals, who had been in the district for three years, had not turned in one supervision of instruction report nor one evaluation for the more than seventy teachers and support staff in his school. I noted in his evaluations that the superintendent had admonished the principal for these failings in each of his evaluations and had, each year, set goals for the principal which included his completion of the supervision of instruction and evaluation reports which were the responsibility of all principals. In my first private meeting with him, we discussed the situation and its' implications for his staff. He agreed that the supervision and evaluation process was very important for everyone and promised me that he would begin fulfilling his professional obligations immediately. I, being the type of administrator who believed that a professional who promised to do something would do it to the best of his ability, accepted his promise and moved on to other important tasks.

At the end of that first year as superintendent, imagine my surprise to establish that the principal had not completed even one supervision of instruction or evaluation report. The chairman of our school board, who was relatively new to the governance of education, was wholly convinced that I had been effective in my new role as superintendent and wrote me a highly complementary evaluation. In only one minor area was he critical in the written report—he felt that I should have dismissed the offending principal and found someone to replace him. When we met to discuss my evaluation, I explained to him that education was not like business—we tended to lean over backwards to give support and assistance, instead of firing an individual for his shortcomings. I insisted that I would work with the principal and ensure that he would fulfill his professional obligations. By the way, he was talented in many other ways, and his school functioned with alacrity.

During my first evaluation meeting with this principal, I insisted that he could no longer neglect the supervision of instruction in his school or the overall evaluation of his teaching and support staffs. He was fully in agreement with me and set his professional goals for the following year with these two responsibilities as his number one and two goals. It is interesting to note that these areas should not have been a part of his professional goal setting, as they were understood responsibilities of the principal's job. Nevertheless, because neither formal supervision nor evaluation had taken place in the school for more than four years, I felt that to formalize these processes as goals would ensure that they were carried out. Circumstances had indeed already occurred where I, as superintendent of the school district, had been called upon to offer formal recommendations for teachers leaving the school. Inasmuch as there had been neither supervision nor evaluation, I was compelled to interview the teachers, and occasionally their colleagues and students, in order to ascertain what could be written into letters of recommendation. (Letters of recommendation, as one can imagine, are significantly important in the recruitment of international teachers, as the recruitment process is extremely time constrained. Teachers are generally offered contracts on the basis of one or two interviews carried out over a weekend. Looking at recommendations and checking with referees are crucial steps in the hiring process.)

During the second year, I met more frequently with the neglectful principal. After each of our meetings, I made personal notes recording the substance of the meetings and any decisions reached. Additionally, I reported the outcomes of the meetings to the chairman of the school board, in order that he would be 'in the picture' regarding my dealings with the principal. Because he did not fully understand the workings of an educational institution, I felt it important to share with him the ongoing developments in relation to my dealings with this principal. (And, the fact that the one negative item in my overall evaluation related to him, I felt I was compelled to keep the chairman informed.)

The meetings with the principal in question went well; he assured me that he was working on the evaluations and that they would be completed by the end of the ensuing school year. It is necessary to note that all other principals, some in schools with even larger staffs than the one in question, were completing their reports and submitting them to the human resources office. Nothing additional was being asked of the high school principal in question. In my final meeting of the year with him, just prior to my finalizing my evaluation report of him, I asked him for the preliminary reports on the supervision of instruction and evaluations. He informed me that he did not have them and that he would submit them to me shortly after the school year ended. I, of course, because of his previous record, became suspicious that nothing had been done. Together with my assistant superintendent of human resources, we interviewed a number of the staff members in the school and confirmed my doubts—no one had been supervised and no evaluation reports had been written.

Anticipating a difficult meeting with the chairman of the school board, I asked for a meeting with the chairman's assistant, an erstwhile superintendent of schools, and enquired what should be done. I suggested that I felt strongly enough after the lies and fabrications received from the principal that I should terminate his employment—in accordance with the evaluation report I had received the previous year. The assistant told me that the most difficult task facing a superintendent was the dismissal of a school administrator who, to most of the parents and students, appeared to be doing his job. He suggested that I put a plan of action into effect with the principal, allowing a period of time equal to a full school year, for him to accomplish his assigned responsibilities and to make it exceedingly clear what the expectations were. I agreed to do this, and before my personal evaluation meeting with the chairman of the board in August of that year, I devised a contract which I presented the principal, outlining the goals and timelines pertaining to his responsibilities in the areas of supervision of instruction and staff evaluation. However, instead of one school year, which I felt was insufficient time for this particular principal to accomplish his goals, I allowed an eighteen month period for him to complete the reports for everyone on his staff. In my evaluation meeting, the chairman of the board complimented me highly for my accomplishments in the role of superintendent and confirmed his evaluation of me in a letter which was also submitted to the board at large. When I explained the steps I had taken with the principal, he applauded my decisions and efforts and supported me in the contract submitted. He also confided in me that he was not a supporter of this particular principal and felt that he was arrogant and unsupportive of the school board. I, quite naively it turns out, assumed that he would share this information with the other members of the school board.

During the beginning of the following school year, I met several times with the principal regarding his contract and goals, and, as per usual, was assured that he was making great inroads in the evaluation of his staff. In fact, in October of that year, he submitted formal evaluations for the three counsellors working in his school. Success! These were the first formal evaluations submitted for any of the staff of that school since it had been instituted four years earlier. I complimented the principal on his efforts, but told him that the terms of his contract demanded that all members of the staff be evaluated before the end of the school year in June. We reviewed the terms of the contract, which included that his formal working contract with our school district would be terminated if indeed he did not accomplish the tasks as laid out. Again, he agreed with me and told me that he had made the supervision of instruction a priority and was working hard to accomplish the goals. Of course, in education, working hard on a goal is oftentimes enough to delay actions for not completing a goal—a circumstance which this principal understood very well.

In the middle of November, I met again with the principal in his office. In this meeting, I asked him to show me the results of his supervision of instruction to date, in order that I could see how he was accomplishing the task and how far he had progressed in the completion of what is a long, time-consuming process. He refused, saying that he had nothing to show me. At that juncture, I asked him point-blank if he would accomplish the goals set forward in his contract with me. He, as was his wont, waffled and suggested that he would be attempting to complete the work that was his responsibility. He then asked me if I intended to renew his working contract when it expired in June. I responded in the negative, indicating that there was absolutely no evidence that he was fulfilling his contractual obligations in the areas of supervision of instruction and teacher/staff evaluation. He immediately became angry; he began yelling at me and demanded that I leave his office. He implied that I had always "...had it in for him..." and that I had continued to pick on him from the day, three and one half years earlier, when I had become superintendent. As I left the office, he shouted that I would soon hear more from him regarding this issue! No kidding!

After writing my notes summarizing the meeting, I immediately contacted the chairman of the board and shared with him the circumstances of our meeting. *He chuckled and said that he would have loved to have been a fly on the wall during that exchange!* I assumed that he understood the nature of the meeting as well as the implications of what this would eventually mean for the school district—a new principal search to replace this administrator. He assured me that it was definitely long overdue that someone else administers to student and faculty needs in that school.

Within three or four days, the chairman of the board called me in the evening and, in a voice laced with ominous tones, told me that "we" had a problem. When I inquired as to what that problem might be, he informed me that the board had received a grievance against me, filed by the principal, indicating that I had threatened him for no reason with the loss of his job. I was not surprised, but it did seem odd to me that the chairman of the board seemed somehow to see this as a threat. I was secure in the knowledge that all of the issues surrounding this situation had been recorded by me, reported repeatedly to the chairman of the school board and that all steps in the procedure had been accomplished within the guidelines set by school board policies.

The next evening, one of the board committees (finance) had a regularly scheduled meeting. During the course of the meeting, a member asked if we could hold an 'ad hoc' meeting later that evening to discuss the issue of the grievance filed against me. Later that evening, in the 'ad hoc' meeting, one of the board members asked me to explain what the essence of this grievance was. I explained in detail the events of the previous four years which had led to the grievance in question. The members of the committee expressed surprise that such procedural issues as this had led to the filing of a grievance, implying that this was the first time they had heard of the situation. Looking at the chairman of the board for support, I explained that I had, in addition to reporting the process in detail to the chairman, put all of the detail of the process in personal notes. One of the members asked if he could see my notes. As we were meeting in the board room next to my office, I was able to retrieve the binder in which I had detailed the events and circumstances relating to this incident, and I, without hesitation, handed them over to this member. (This was the last time I ever saw my notes; they were never returned to me. Fortunately, I had made copies of most of my confidential files, and therefore had copies of the notes which I could refer to in the future.)

As the procedures for filing a grievance were laid out in district policy and they were very clear, the process was immediately laid out for the board and me to proceed. Again, because I had been aware of and in compliance with the procedures and guidelines as laid out in policy, I was hardly uncomfortable regarding the outcome of the grievance. Mr. Naivety!

On Saturday morning, I met with the chairman of the board and his vice-chairperson. They explained to me that the board felt awkward about releasing the principal in question. They asked me again to explain my reasoning and to assure them that all policies and procedures had been followed. At the end of the meeting, they asked if I could be persuaded to allow the principal another year to conform to the district policies regarding supervision of instruction and evaluation. I demurred, indicating that I would do whatever I was instructed to do, but until the grievance was appropriately dealt with, I was compelled to stand by my policy-driven procedures. A look passed from the chairman to his assistant and I believed that they would deal with the grievance post haste.

During the following couple of days (actually Saturday and Sunday, but because we were in Saudi Arabia, these were regular work days...), the board met on more than one occasion. I was not invited to these meetings, which I found somewhat strange as the grievance was levelled at me and policy allowed for me to explain my side of the situation. Nevertheless, I was never to meet with the board again.

On Sunday evening, I had the meeting already described with parents from ARAMCO, their concern naturally being the issue regarding the Ministry of Education's directive disallowing their children to attend our high school. Even though I had not yet been given the go ahead to officially state that the directive was being rescinded, I was told that I could assure these parents that they had nothing to worry about. The issue would be eliminated and their children would be allowed to attend our school. As the meeting ended, the parents swarmed me at the front of the room to shake my hand and express their appreciation for the denouement of their concern. While I was meeting with these parents, the board held a meeting with the principal and his wife—presumably to hear their concerns and detail regarding the grievance.

The next morning, as I worked at my desk, a board member came into my office and handed me a copy of a letter that had been sent to the principal. The letter stated that the grievance had been studied and an investigation had determined that the grievance had no substance and was therefore dropped. I felt a wave of relief sweep over me and was pleased by this outcome. I anticipated a further meeting with the board to finalize their concerns and to hear what they wished for me to do. As the chairman had indicated in our Friday meeting, I expected the board to instruct me to allow the principal another year to fulfill the obligations of his contract. Of course, while this would be what I believed to be an exception to board policy, I was wholly prepared to follow whichever course of action the board instructed.

Late that afternoon, the board chairman entered my office with a newly appointed member of the board (I had carried out an introduction to the board and its duties with this man the previous week.) The chairman handed me a sealed envelope and asked me to read the letter contained within. I opened the letter and began reading I had been released! Effective immediately! When I caught my breath, I looked at the chairman and asked what the reason for this drastic action was. He responded that I should read the letter again; everything was contained therein. I suggested that I had not had a chance to speak with the board as a whole and that, in interest of the operation of the school district and my personal interests as well as those of my family; I would like to have the opportunity to speak with the board. I pointed out that my wife's contract was also being terminated, and as far as I knew, she had had nothing to do with the decision they had met regarding me. He refused the request, stating that the decision had been finalized and we had precisely nineteen days to leave the Kingdom! One could have knocked me over with a feather! This was the same man whom I had worked with from my first day in the superintendent's office and the person I had confided in, worked closely with, and whose admonitions regarding the principal in question I had followed! As I protested the unprofessionalism and unfairness of the circumstance, he relented and confirmed that he would meet with me and my wife in ten days' time, after he had returned from a business trip. He stated that such a meeting would have no chance of altering the board's decision, but that he would hear what we had to say. With that, he and the board member stood and left my office.

That evening, after my wife and our two children discussed the terms of my dismissal (our children were essentially being expelled from school; our daughter was the top academic student in her class and had been the complete time she attended that school; she had served as the secretary/treasurer of the students' council and was in the Honour Society; she had also been the most valuable player on the soccer and volleyball teams; our son was a senior and was beginning the final semester of his high school years; all of his friends would graduate without him; both of our children would be compelled to leave all of their friends behind), I called an emergency meeting for all school and district office administrators in my home. In the meeting I explained that I had been released from my duties and that I would no longer be allowed to work with them. I was unable to answer their questions, in particular, why was I being released? I read the letter of dismissal to them and told them that was all the information I had been given.

The next several days were a nightmare. Our children suffered the most; there were student demonstrations and walkouts. Students wanted an explanation—almost as much as I and my family desired one. My son stood up in a student assembly—was forced to defend his father and mother to questions from the floor questioning what it was that his parents had done wrong. He was only able to tell them that his parents had done nothing wrong and that further explanations from the board for their actions were not forthcoming. As I think back to the turmoil of those days, I can't imagine a school board being as callous and uncaring as to force two outstanding students and citizens from their school—without so much as a comforting message. The days and evenings were filled with tears and suffering in our home.

Of course, over the course of the next several days I attempted to call members of the board. None of them would talk to me! Secretaries and spouses were told to deny all requests from me to speak to the members. I was put on hold and eventually denied any contact with them. Unbelievable!

Finally, the vice-chairperson whose guidance I had sought so many months before regarding the principal's short-comings and whose suggestions I had followed closely, agreed to meet with me and my wife. We met in the district offices one evening; he began the meeting by stating that he would listen to our concerns but that he had been instructed to answer no questions. I, and then my wife, each spoke for several minutes. We demonstrated our absolute astonishment and surprise at the decisions that had been taken and asked for an explanation. True to his word, no explanation was forthcoming. He would not answer our questions; however, during the last several minutes of the meeting he cried visibly—tears running down his cheeks and staining his blue broadcloth shirt, a visual that I will never forget. It was pretty obvious to us that he understood the damage being done to us and our children. The meeting was heartbreaking.

Five days later, we met with the chairman and vice-chairman again in an evening meeting. As in the previous meeting, we were told that they were there to listen to our concerns but that no questions would be answered and no decisions would be altered. So, my final meeting in an educational setting was a 'fait accompli'. After more than forty years of dedicating my personal and professional life to education, I was offered nothing but an ear. As an addendum to the insulting manner in which I and my family were treated, I learned later that an agreement had been made behind my back for one of my assistant superintendents to become the superintendent! All professionalism aside, this person did not have the professional loyalty or the personal integrity to discuss the circumstances with me, but kept her involvement hidden. In fact, it was not until several months later that I learned of her deception and unprofessional conduct.

In fairness, I must mention that the board paid out our contracts. The previous spring I had requested a two-year extension on my contract as our daughter would have two more years in high school before she graduated. We as a family had agreed that once our daughter finished school, I would retire from the professional life in education. The board had, in a letter praising me for my dedication, accomplishments and industry, offered me the requested two-year extension. This particular letter of recommendation and evaluation was completed in August, just six weeks before my release. In the letter releasing me, they had noted that the requested contract extension had been rescinded. However, our existing contracts were in force through June and the board paid our salaries to the end of the contract. Also there were no penalties assigned to us and we received our accumulated pension allotments and shipping allowances. Had I truly done something untoward that was the impetus for our release, it is obvious that we would not have been paid these significant sums of money and our contracts would have been terminated. Not only that, this board said in the letter that they would provide letters of recommendation in order that we could look for future employment!

We were able to get our lives together in the nineteen days allotted us (board policy allowed everyone under contract a minimum of thirty days) and leave the Kingdom. We decided to only sell our vehicles and to give all other possessions away. Items such as our pool table, television sets and kitchen appliances were simply given to our children's friends or to the workers who had helped to make our lives bearable while living in the Kingdom. Just a week before Christmas, we flew from Saudi

Arabia for the last time and found ourselves back in Canada. I retired from education at the age of sixty-five years.

Some Final Thoughts

International education, as you can see, brings a large and varied number of experiences to the table that one doesn't encounter in public education. Public school experience had taught me to deal with death, violence, thievery, drugs and alcohol in school, but had not prepared me for the unique experiences of the international educator. International schools are all different; many persons assume that they can all be defined under one heading, but in fact, because they are located in diverse countries all over the world, they are significantly different. No matter where one accepts international school positions, the varying laws and cultures dictate unique school experiences. As I have described, everything from bribery to government interference to security in the face of terrorism is considered normal. Learning to understand and cope with such a wide range of differing circumstances requires dedication, long hours and patience. As was my experience in public education administration, most training took place on the job and under fire—there was little or no training available anywhere for the prospective international administrator.

Most international schools are managed by a superintendent or director, the person who is responsible to the governing board. The superintendent, in addition to overseeing the education of children, must annually recruit teachers and school administrators (a fifteen to twenty-five percent annual turnover of staff is generally expected), deal with government requirements, ensure the security and safety of all staff and students, react to whatever disruptions occur in the school and community, appease disgruntled and frustrated parents, ensure reasonable contracts and working conditions for all employees and report monthly to the board of directors (school board). School boards often consist of persons who have little understanding of the needs of elementary and secondary education; too often members are influential business people representing the human resource needs of their own companies, or parents who have personal axes to grind regarding their children and the school. Naturally all boards include persons of integrity and dedication; unfortunately too often their influence is weakened because of most boards' required focus on the costs of education.

Having said this, the quality of international education is outstanding. As an international administrator, I was always proud of the student outcomes which reflected so positively on the schools. It was not uncommon to hear teachers comment on their international teaching experiences as being the epitome of their professional careers—that they were finally able to accomplish the goals they had set when they originally decided to enter the field of education. They no longer were compelled to focus on discipline and behavioural issues, but were able to concentrate on the teaching of children. There is no better recommendation for international education.

It is with fondness and pride that I recount my more than forty years of experience in public and international education. I consider myself fortunate to have had such a wide variety of experiences and opportunities to work with students and teachers. It is still a pleasure to meet ex-students and teachers in the grocery store, on the street and at public functions and to have them comment positively on our associations of bygone years. If I had it all to do over, knowing what I know now, I would do it all again—but be better prepared.

So, what do you think? Do you really want to be a principal?

www.ingramcontent.com/pod-product-compliance
Lightning Source LLC
LaVergne TN
LVHW041812060526
838201LV00046B/1234